Nosthimia!

Cooking with Georgia
FOR THE FINEST
IN GREEK AMERICAN COOKING

Georgia

HAPPY COOKING
www.georgiasrealfood.com

NEW AMERICAN FAMILY COOKBOOKS

Nosthimia!

The Greek American Family Cookbook

GEORGIA SARIANIDES

CAPITAL BOOKS, INC.

STERLING, VIRGINIA

Capital Books, Inc.
P.O. Box 605
Herndon, Virginia 20172-0605

Photos by Georgia Sarianides, Peter Sarianides, Morea, and the Greek National Tourism Organization.

Book composition by Coghill Composition Company, Richmond, Virginia

ISBN 1-931868-73-5 (alk.paper)

Library of Congress Cataloging-in-Publication Data

Sarianides, Georgia.
    Nosthimia! : the Greek American family cookbook / Georgia Sarianides.— 1st ed.
        p.   cm.— (New American family cookbooks)
    ISBN 1-931868-73-5 (alk. paper)
    1. Cookery, Greek.   I. Title.   II. Series.
  TX723.5.G8838   2004
  641.59495—dc22

2003025266

Printed in the United States of America on acid-free paper that meets the American National Standards Institute Z39-48 Standard.

First Edition

10 9 8 7 6 5 4 3 2 1

CONTENTS

ACKNOWLEDGMENTS vii

INTRODUCTION ix

Appetizers 1

General Food Tips 31

Soups 35

Greek Herbs and Spices 49

Salads 53

Greek Olives 63

Dressings and Sauces 65

Greek Cheeses 75

Vegetarian Dishes 79

Olive Oil 100

Chicken Dishes 103

Red-Dyed Eggs for Easter 125

Main Dishes 127

The Olympic Games: A Time to
    Celebrate Greece 175

Seafood Dishes 179

Fillo Dough Directions and Tips 201

Pasta and Rice Dishes 203

Greek Spirits 217

Pizzas and Calzones 221

Pies and Tarts 235

Desserts 255

INDEX 285

ACKNOWLEDGMENTS

*T*his book is dedicated to my loving daughter and son, Despina and Peter Sarianides. Without their love and support and their extraordinarily hard work, this book would never have been possible. It is also dedicated to my irreplaceable husband, Peter, for his love and caring throughout this long culinary adventure. And, to my sons, John and George, I thank you for your patience and help. Finally, thanks and love to my parents, Margarita and John Liakopoulos, for always allowing me to be me and to pursue my love of cooking.

A number of people have helped turn my dream into a book that actually sits on the shelves of bookstores and kitchens around the world. Thanks to my agent, Kirsten Kelly, and my editor, Noemi C. Arthur; the Greek National Tourist Organization for the pictures of Greece that have helped the book come alive; Jenny Noures Photography for photographs of me and my Greek dishes; Hellas International, Inc., for photographs; Chris Radant for writing special projects; and a special thanks to LS Management Company, which has made all of this possible, and my baby sister, Grigoria Liakopoulos, for thinking of the book's title, *Nosthimia.*

And thanks to you, my readers and fans, who have been a source of encouragement as I walked the bumpy road of fulfilling my lifelong dream. You have showered me with e-mails and letters thanking me for my recipes and filling me with a sense of purpose and resolve. I hope you will come to know me through my food and to understand my wish to share the healthy and delicious cuisine of my native Greece. It is also my wish to help you serve these wonderful dishes without spending a lot of time in the kitchen. For I, too, am an American, a Greek American, and I know how hectic life can be.

Georgia's four children (left to right): Daisy, Peter, John, and George

INTRODUCTION

Food, family, and love—where I come from, it's all the same. So welcome to my family!
—GEORGIA SARIANIDES

W hen you cook together, you share a part of your-self. And since I am Greek, I want to share as much as possible. This is how we are. I even wish I could share being Greek with you, because I feel so lucky to have been born in such a beautiful place.

I come from a small town, called Amaliada, in Peloponnese in the sunny south of Greece. This area is a part of the Greek mainland, but is separated from the mainland by the Gulf of Corinth. Just a tiny isthmus attaches it to the rest of Greece, so its residents tend to stay there and grow up together as an entire community. Life there is hospitable, friendly, beautiful, bountiful, and warm in every way. The landscape varies from the most massive oak- and pine-covered mountains to the beautiful clear blue of the sky reflected in the Adriatic Sea. The climate itself is delicious. The sun gives its warmth to the trees; the trees bear fruit to pass the

A street in Peloponnese, Greece.

warmth to the Greek people. And the Greek people love to share that warmth by cooking and eating with loved ones.

Everything in Greece revolves around food. The holidays involve fasting and feasting; weddings, funerals, everything is celebrated with healthy, hardy, mouthwatering food. We grew up eating the best olive oil and herbs, fresh fruit, homemade cheeses, and wine like you find nowhere else in the world. My mother made the yogurt and feta, marinated the olives, and baked bread. My father grew much of what we ate on our farm, and he made the wine, ground the wheat flour, and harvested olives.

There were six girls in my family and one boy, who was certain he was a king. I was the sixth child born, so I had only my little sister to boss around. Each of us had a favorite dish that our mother would prepare: Takis always favored lentil soup, Despina had a sweet tooth and begged Mama to make kourambiethes. As Despina got older, she made them almost every day. And not for the whole family—she could eat them all by herself. Don't ask how she remains thin to this day.

The Major Feast Days

Nativity of the Theotokos	September 8
Exaltation of the Holy Cross	September 14
Presentation of the Theotokos in the Temple	November 21
Christmas (Nativity of Jesus Christ)	December 25
Epiphany (Baptism of Christ)	January 6
Presentation of Christ in the Temple	February 2
Annunciation (Evangelismos)	March 25
Easter (Pascha)	(Varies from year to year)
Ascension	(40 days after Easter)
Pentecost	(50 days after Easter)
Transfiguration of Christ	August 6
Dormition of the Theotokos (Kimissis)	August 15

There is no justice. Demitras's dish was pasta, and, of course, the variations are endless. Sofia loved chicken with noodles. Moussaka was Andiana's pleasure, and Grigoria always asked for rice. My absolute favorite was bread with feta and olive oil with salt and pepper, but I wanted to taste everything. I remember being quite frustrated with my sister, Grigoria, because she always wanted rice for lunch. This bored me to tears. Finally, I had to threaten her so she wouldn't continue to ask for it. In retrospect, it's easy to see where my cooking urges were born. From the time I was little, I knew there were so many delicious things.

To accommodate all of us, Mama spent a lot of time in the kitchen. And that's where I stayed—right by her side. I loved to observe her while she worked. I would ask, "Mama how do you make these things?" And she would say, "Just watch, don't ask." These are some of my fondest memories, watching her concentration and her joy at knowing how these delicious fresh foods complemented one another. It was magic, and I was able to learn it. My mother was my role model. People say we have exactly the same personality, which makes me feel so proud.

My father has always been my hero. He's a quiet, peaceful man who never raised his voice except to laugh. And it's no wonder he was peaceful—he was well fed, got lots of exercise (then referred to as "living"), and was surrounded by his children and wife who adored him. I'm still daddy's little girl, even though he is now ninety-two and I have been smaller in my time.

Georgia's parents, John and Margarita Liakopoulos, Greece, 1954.

It's calming to live in accord with nature and with tradition. Literally, we ate, drank, and slept our Greek-ness. Nothing separated us from the land we lived on. We felt safe because we were steeped in traditions that our ancestors followed. Even our superstitions made us feel invincible. We were very old-fashioned. My father was always seated first. Everyone had a glass of wine with dinner, and the food was always fresh, healthful, and delicious—grown right there in the same place we grew up.

In Greece, the Christmas liturgy is performed on Christmas Eve around midnight. When the liturgy is over and the parishioners return home, many families eat chicken soup with egg and lemon, Christmas bread, and pastries, such as kourambiethes and baklava. The traditional Christmas dinner is stuffed turkey. I remember the smells of dinner and all the activity in the kitchen. Every year, we celebrated with a wonderful meal that we had anticipated for weeks in advance. There were no lavish gifts as there are today, but our father gave us each two drachmas, the equivalent of about two dollars, and we were thrilled. We felt like the luckiest and most loved children in the world.

For forty days before Pascha, or Greek Easter, we gave up eating meat and dairy. On Easter, there was a feast of lamb, or lamb soup, called mageritsa, flaounes, which are Easter cakes, and tsoureki—a sweet bread made with egg in the middle.

A wonderful New Year's tradition was to make "lucky bread," or vassilopita, named after St. Vasili. A coin was baked inside the bread, and whoever got the slice with the coin was convinced he or she had a year of great luck ahead.

I have been fortunate to have many lucky years, each following the one before it. I came to America just a young girl without knowing a word of English. And now I am able to share my love of food and family with thousands of people of every nationality.

I was born and raised in Greece but I am an American now, a Greek American. In the Old Country, we used lots of butter and oil and spent hours preparing meals. But Americans are busy and health conscious, and I want my recipes to help them prepare easy and nutritious meals that fit their lifestyle. My recipes are the best of both worlds: Greek with an American twist, just like me.

Do I miss my homeland? To this day, every time I eat my favorite childhood snack—toasted bread drizzled with olive oil and salt and pepper—it takes me back to those happy days with my family in Greece. Now I have my own husband and children, and I share these same traditions, pleasures, and principles with them. Together as a family, we bring them to you with love, from the heart of our home.

Georgia and Daisy.

Nosthimia!

Appetizers

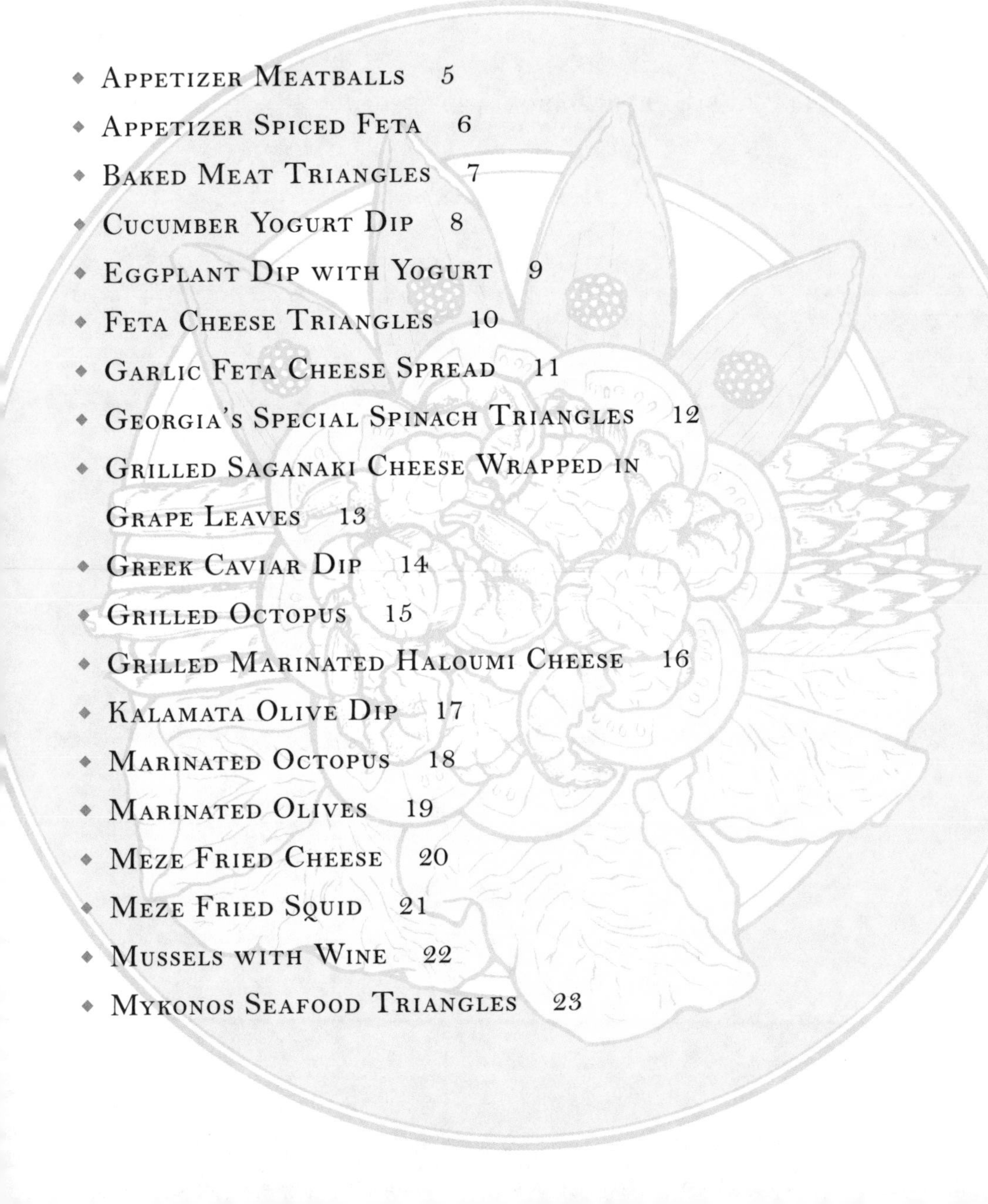

- Appetizer Meatballs   5
- Appetizer Spiced Feta   6
- Baked Meat Triangles   7
- Cucumber Yogurt Dip   8
- Eggplant Dip with Yogurt   9
- Feta Cheese Triangles   10
- Garlic Feta Cheese Spread   11
- Georgia's Special Spinach Triangles   12
- Grilled Saganaki Cheese Wrapped in Grape Leaves   13
- Greek Caviar Dip   14
- Grilled Octopus   15
- Grilled Marinated Haloumi Cheese   16
- Kalamata Olive Dip   17
- Marinated Octopus   18
- Marinated Olives   19
- Meze Fried Cheese   20
- Meze Fried Squid   21
- Mussels with Wine   22
- Mykonos Seafood Triangles   23

◆ OLIVE AND CHEESE PLATTER   24

◆ POTATOES WITH GARLIC SAUCE   25

◆ GEORGIA'S SHRIMP WITH FETA IN FILLO   26

◆ SHRIMP WITH GARLIC   27

◆ TOASTED BREAD RIGANATO WITH TOMATOES
AND FETA   28

◆ YIAYIA'S GARLIC SAUCE   29

*M*eze (appetizers) are typically served with the famous Greek aperitif, ouzo, which is made from grape stems and flavored with aniseed. Meze is usually translated as "appetizers" or "starters," but this translation does not do justice to the underlying role meze play in Greek tradition. Taverns in Greece are swamped with people drinking ouzo, and the same people nibble on an assortment of small plates of meze.

The ancient Greeks made it impossible for their society to indulge in alcohol without something tasty to nibble on. They knew that drinking on an empty stomach was not a sensible idea, so it became mandatory to serve meze wherever alcohol was offered. Since then, meze have become an essential part of Greek social life. With or without alcohol, you can always find an assortment of meze on the table.

Meze can be anything from a few marinated olives or a small piece of cheese to platters loaded with different dips, fish, octopus, fried squid, smelts, and little savory fillo triangles. In this chapter I include some of my favorite meze to enjoy with your family and friends.

A dinner table set with appetizers and other dishes.

Appetizer Meatballs

FRIED KEFTEDHES

Fried keftethakia are the most popular appetizers in Greece. Many people serve them as a main course with a salad and fried potatoes. This delicious treat tastes great hot or cold.

1½ pounds lean ground beef

½ cup plain bread crumbs

1 large onion, grated

3 cloves garlic, finely chopped

1 egg, slightly beaten

2 tablespoons finely chopped
    fresh parsley

1 tablespoon finely chopped
    fresh mint

1 teaspoon dried oregano

2 tablespoons freshly squeezed
    lemon juice

Salt and pepper

¾ to 1 cup flour

½ cup olive oil, for frying
    the meatballs

Mix meat, bread crumbs, grated onion, garlic, egg, parsley, mint, oregano, lemon juice, salt, and pepper in a large bowl. Knead all of the ingredients very well, then cover and refrigerate for 1 hour. Shape 1 tablespoon of meat mixture into a small meatball. Dredge meatballs in flour, then add oil to a large, heavy skillet and heat it until it's almost smoking. Fry kaftethakia a few at a time, turning them constantly until brown. Serve hot or cold.

◆ *Yields 2 to 2½ dozen*

Appetizer Spiced Feta

MEZE ME FETA

1 pound feta cheese

1 teaspoon dried oregano

1 tablespoon chopped fresh thyme

3 cloves garlic, finely chopped

Juice of ½ lemon

¼ cup olive oil

Freshly ground pepper

Rinse the feta with cold water and pat dry. Cut it into large cubes and place them in a bowl. In small jar mix oregano, thyme, garlic, lemon juice, olive oil, and pepper. Pour marinade over the feta and mix well. This is delicious with crusty bread and ouzo.

◆ *Serves 6*

Baked Meat Triangles

Bourekakia me Kima

These delicious meat-filled fillo dough triangles can be served hot or cold.

¼ cup olive oil

1 large onion, grated

3 cloves garlic, finely chopped

1½ pounds extra-lean ground beef

2 tablespoons chopped fresh parsley

1 tablespoon chopped fresh mint

½ cup white wine

1 teaspoon dried oregano

½ teaspoon allspice

Salt and pepper

½ cup kefalotyri or Parmesan cheese, grated

2 tablespoons plain bread crumbs

1 teaspoon paprika

½ cup pine nuts

1 pound fillo dough

Preheat the oven to 350 degrees. In a medium saucepan, heat olive oil and sauté the onion and garlic for 3 minutes or until soft. Add ground beef and cook, stirring, until the meat is browned. Add parsley, mint, wine, oregano, allspice, salt, and pepper. Reduce the heat to medium and cook for 15 to 20 minutes, until the liquid has evaporated. Remove the pan from the heat and add the kefalotyri cheese, bread crumbs, paprika, and pine nuts. Mix all the ingredients together well and allow the mixture cool for 25 to 30 minutes before continuing. Follow the directions for making the tiropitakia triangles of the fillo dough (see page 201).

◆ *Yields 2 to 2½ dozen*

Cucumber Yogurt Dip

Tzatziki

Tzatziki is a popular Greek dip. It is served with souvlaki, lamb, pork, chicken, or vegetables. Tzatziki is also low in calories.

1 container (16 ounces) plain yogurt

1 large cucumber, peeled, grated, and drained

4 cloves garlic, minced

1 tablespoon finely chopped dill (optional)

3 tablespoons olive oil

1 tablespoon white vinegar

Salt to taste

Dill or parsley, for garnish (optional)

Drain yogurt into a cheesecloth-lined colander, tie the ends of the cloth together, and place in the refrigerator for 5 to 6 hours until the yogurt is strained and thickened. Place the yogurt in a medium bowl. Place the peeled and grated cucumber in cheesecloth and squeeze until all the water is removed; then add the cucumber to the yogurt. Add the garlic, dill, olive oil, white vinegar, and salt. Mix all the ingredients well; sprinkle with dill, then cover and refrigerate until ready to serve.

♦ *Yields 2 cups*

Eggplant Dip with Yogurt

MELIZANOSALATA

Serve this delicious dip with bread or crackers. It can also be served as a side dish.

2 to 3 large eggplants

3 cloves garlic, minced

¼ cup olive oil

Juice of 1 lemon

1 medium onion, grated

Salt and pepper

1½ cups plain yogurt, drained

2 tablespoons finely chopped flat parsley

2 to 3 tablespoons bread crumbs

Parsley, for garnish

Preheat the oven to 375 degrees. Wash the eggplants and pat dry, then pierce them with a fork. Bake them for about 1 hour, inserting a fork to check them for tenderness (they should be soft). Remove the skin and seeds and process the eggplants in a food processor until they form a smooth pulp. Continue processing and add the garlic, oil, lemon, and onion. Sprinkle with salt and pepper and keep processing until the dip mixture becomes very light. Place the mixture in a large bowl, then add the yogurt, parsley, and bread crumbs and stir well. Cover and refrigerate for 2 hours before serving. Garnish with parsley.

◆ *Serves 6*

Feta Cheese Triangles

TIROPITAKIA

This delicious appetizer is great for any occasion.

1 pound feta cheese, crumbled

½ cup crumbled goat cheese

½ cup grated kefalotyri or
   Parmesan cheese

2 eggs, well beaten

¼ cup milk

Freshly ground pepper

Pinch of nutmeg

1 pound fillo dough

Olive oil, for brushing fillo dough

Preheat the oven to 350 degrees. In a large bowl, combine feta, goat cheese, and kefalotyri. In a small bowl, beat the eggs well and add the milk, pepper, and nutmeg, then add to the cheese mixture and mix very well with a fork. To prepare the triangles, see page 201.

◆ *Yields about 3 dozen*

Garlic Feta Cheese Spread

FETA KOPANISTI

This delicious spread is served as a meze (appetizer) with crusty bread or pita bread and ouzo. I love it!

1 pound feta cheese, crumbled

3 cloves garlic, minced

1 medium sweet Italian pepper, finely chopped

¼ cup olive oil, plus 1 teaspoon for drizzling

1 medium dried red mild chili pepper, finely chopped (optional)

½ teaspoon dried thyme

1 teaspoon dried oregano

Juice of 1 lemon

Freshly ground pepper to taste

Pinch of paprika

Into a food processor, add the feta, garlic, pepper, oil, chili pepper, thyme, oregano, lemon, and pepper to taste. Purée until feta is smooth and creamy. Put the spread into a bowl, drizzle the top with olive oil, and sprinkle with paprika. Cover and refrigerate until serving.

◆ *Yields 1¾ to 2 cups*

Georgia's Special Spinach Triangles

SPANAKOPITAKIA

Spanakopitakia is one of the most popular Greek meze. It can be served hot or cold.

2 to 2½ pounds fresh spinach

1 cup olive oil

1 large onion, finely chopped

½ cup chopped scallions

½ cup chopped fresh parsley

½ cup chopped fresh dill

2 large eggs

½ pound feta cheese, crumbled

½ cup grated kefalotyri or Parmesan cheese

Salt and pepper

1 pound fillo dough

Olive oil, for brushing onto the triangles

Preheat the oven to 350 degrees. Wash the spinach very well and drain it in a colander. When it has drained completely, chop the spinach very thin. In a large saucepan, heat ½ cup olive oil and sauté the onion, scallions, dill, and parsley for 5 minutes. Add the spinach and stir the mixture together. Lower the heat and let simmer for 10 to 15 minutes. Transfer the mixture to a colander to drain any liquid, then place spinach mixture into a large bowl and allow it to cool for 20 minutes. In a medium bowl, beat the eggs, stir in the feta cheese, sprinkle with the grated kefalotyri and a little salt and pepper, and mix the ingredients well. Unroll the fillo dough and keep it covered while working with 2 sheets at a time. Brush each one with oil, then stack one on top of the other. Cut the fillo into 5 long strips. Place 2 teaspoons of the spinach mixture in the middle bottom of each strip, then fold the right corner up and to the left, to form a right angle. Continue folding like a flag, making each into a triangle. Place the triangles 1 inch apart on a greased cookie sheet. Brush the tops with oil and sprinkle with a little water. Bake for about 25 minutes or until they're golden brown.

◆ *Yield 2 to 2½ dozen*

Note: Freeze uncooked spanakopitakia and bake it at another time.

Grilled Saganaki Cheese Wrapped in Grape Leaves

Saganaki me Klematofilla

This is the most delicious meze. I love the flavors of the grilled grape leaves and melted cheese.

1 pound kefalotyri or feta cheese, cut into 2 × 1-inch pieces

3 tablespoons olive oil

Juice of 1 lemon

3 cloves garlic, minced

½ teaspoon dried oregano

Freshly ground pepper

1 16-ounce jar grape leaves

Lemon wedges, for garnish

Preheat the grill. Place the cheese pieces on a large platter and sprinkle them with the olive oil, lemon juice, garlic, oregano, and pepper. Rinse a half-bunch of grape leaves with water, trim off the stems, and pat dry. Take 2 grape leaves and place 1 piece of the cheese in the center. Fold the sides over the cheese and roll up the leaves to form a packet. Repeat with the remaining cheese and grape leaves. Refrigerate the saganaki for 1 hour. Brush each packet with oil and grill over low heat on both sides for a total of 15 minutes. Transfer to a platter and serve hot with toasted Greek flat pita bread or pita pockets cut into wedges. Garnish with lemon wedges.

◆ *Serves 5 to 6*

Greek Caviar Dip

TARAMASALATA

Taramasalata is a traditional Greek dip, made primarily during Lent, but delicious at any time. Serve it with crusty bread, pita, or crackers.

½ loaf Italian white bread

¼ cup tarama (raw carp caviar)

2 medium potatoes, boiled
(reserve some of the water in
which potatoes were boiled)

½ cup chopped scallions, white
part only

½ cup olive oil

Juice of 2 lemons

1 tablespoon chopped fresh flat
parsley, for garnish

5 to 6 kalamata olives, for garnish

Cut the crust off the bread, then drizzle the bread with water and squeeze it to remove excess moisture. In a food processor, combine the bread, tarama, potatoes, and scallions and pulse for 2 minutes. Slowly add the olive oil and lemon juice and continue pulsing until the mixture is creamy. Place the mixture in a medium bowl, sprinkle it with parsley and garnish with olives, then cover and chill it until serving.

♦ Yields 1½ to 2 cups

Note: If the dip appears to be too thick, add some of the liquid used to boil the potatoes.

Grilled Octopus

KTAPODI PSITO STA KARVOUNA

Octopus is a Greek delicacy. Serve it as a hot or cold appetizer with crusty bread and ouzo or wine.

2 to 3 pounds fresh or frozen
   octopus
½ cup red wine vinegar
½ cup olive oil
1 teaspoon dried oregano
1 teaspoon chopped fresh rosemary

3 cloves garlic, minced
2 bay leaves, crushed
Salt and pepper
Juice of 1 lemon
Parsley, for garnish

Wash the octopus very well, then put it in a large pot and cover with cold water. Bring the octopus to a boil and cook it over medium heat for 1 hour, or until the flesh is pierced easily with a fork. Remove from the pot, rinse with cold water, and place in a large bowl. In a medium bowl, mix the vinegar, oil, oregano, rosemary, garlic, bay leaves, salt, and pepper. Pour the mixture over the octopus; cover and refrigerate it overnight. Preheat the grill, then put the octopus in a grill basket and grill it for 15 minutes on each side. Cut up the grilled octopus and sprinkle it with some oil and lemon juice. Garnish with parsley.

◆ *Serves 4*

Grilled Marinated Haloumi Cheese

HALOUMI STA KARVOUNA

This is a delicious appetizer. Haloumi cheese is produced in Cyprus.

1 pound haloumi cheese, cut into
   ½-inch slices
3 tablespoons olive oil
1 tablespoon ouzo or 2
   tablespoons white wine
1 tablespoon chopped fresh oregano

Juice of 1 lemon
1 teaspoon chopped fresh thyme
2 cloves garlic, minced
Ground black pepper
Lemon slices and thyme sprigs,
   for garnish

Arrange the cheese slices on a platter and sprinkle them with olive oil, ouzo or wine, oregano, lemon juice, thyme, garlic, and pepper. Marinate for at least 1 hour, preheat the grill, and grill the cheese slices on both sides until lightly browned. Remove from the grill and garnish with lemon slices and thyme. This can be served with salad or roasted eggplants.

◆ *Serves 4*

Kalamata Olive Dip

ELIES KOPANISTES

This dip is a family favorite from my mother's kitchen.

1 pound kalamata olives, pitted
  and chopped
1 onion, chopped
3 cloves garlic, chopped
1 tablespoon chopped fresh mint
Juice of 1 lemon

1 teaspoon dried oregano
½ teaspoon dried basil
3 tablespoons olive oil
Fresh mint or parsley, chopped,
  for garnish

Rinse the olives 2 or 3 times and drain them. In the food processor, add all ingredients and blend for 2 minutes or more, until a smooth paste forms. Place the dip to a medium bowl, garnish with chopped mint or parsley, then cover and refrigerate it (it will stay good for 4 to 5 days). Spread on crusty bread or pita bread.

◆ *Yields 1¼ cups*

Marinated Octopus

KTAPODI MARINARA

This is the best meze—great with a shot of ouzo.

2½ to 3 pounds octopus

1 teaspoon salt

½ cup wine vinegar

¼ cup olive oil

3 cloves garlic, minced

1 bay leaf

1 teaspoon dried oregano

Salt and pepper to taste

Wash the octopus very well and place in a large pot with enough water to cover and 1 teaspoon of salt. Bring to a boil and cook for 50 minutes to 1 hour, or until the flesh pierces easily with a fork. Drain it in a colander, then rinse it with cold water. Cut off the dark skin, then cut the octopus into 1½-inch-long pieces. Place it in a large bowl and add the vinegar, oil, garlic, bay leaf, oregano, and salt and pepper. Mix well to coat the octopus with the marinade. Serve cold as an appetizer or side dish.

♦ *Serves 5*

Marinated Olives

Elies Horiatikes

My mother prepared this delicious recipe using her own olives from the olive trees in our backyard.

1 pound kalamata olives

1 pound green Greek olives

3 to 4 cloves garlic, crushed

1 teaspoon chopped fresh rosemary

1 teaspoon dried oregano

1 ½ teaspoons chopped fresh thyme

1 bay leaf, crushed

1 lemon, sliced

¼ cup red wine vinegar

½ cup olive oil

Place the olives in a colander and rinse with cold water 2 to 3 times. After the water has drained, place the olives in large bowl. In a medium bowl, mix well the garlic, rosemary, oregano, thyme, crushed bay leaf, lemon slices, vinegar, and olive oil. Pour mixture over the olives and stir well. Serve as an appetizer.

♦ *Serves 5 to 6*

Meze Fried Cheese

SAGANAKI

Saganaki is typically served with ouzo and bread.

1 pound kefalotyri cheese or any
   hard yellow cheese
Juice of 1 lemon
½ cup flour
½ teaspoon dried oregano
½ teaspoon dried mint

½ teaspoon paprika
Freshly ground pepper, to taste
½ cup olive oil, to fry cheese
1 tablespoon chopped fresh
   parsley, for garnish
Lemon slices, for garnish

Cut the cheese into strips about 3 inches long and ¾ inch thick. Place the cheese strips on a platter and sprinkle with the lemon juice. In a medium bowl, mix the flour, oregano, mint, paprika, and ground pepper, then dredge the cheese lightly in the flour mixture. Heat oil in a heavy skillet. Add a few pieces of cheese at a time and fry them on both sides for a total of about 3 to 4 minutes, or until golden brown. Arrange on a platter and garnish with parsley and lemon slices.

♦ *Serves 4*

Meze Fried Squid

KALAMARI TIGANITO

Serve this delicious meze hot and squeeze fresh lemon juice over it.

1½ to 2 pounds squid

1 cup flour

¼ cup corn flour

1 cup milk

1 egg

1 cup olive oil or vegetable oil,
    for frying

Juice of 1 lemon

Lemon slices, for garnish

Parsley, for garnish

Rinse the squid 3 to 4 times with cold water, then drain it in a colander. Separate the bodies from tentacles: cut the squid into ¾-inch round rings, leaving the tentacles whole. Mix the flours. In a large bowl, beat the eggs and milk for 5 minutes. Place some of the squid into a strainer, dip the squid into the egg mixture, then dredge it in the flour mixture, making sure to remove any excess flour. In a large skillet, heat the oil until very hot and fry the squid, a few pieces at a time, until crisp and golden brown. Remove the squid and drain it on paper towels. Sprinkle the squid with the lemon juice and garnish it with lemon slices and parsley.

♦ *Serves 4 to 5*

Mussels with Wine

MYTHIA ME KRASI

2½ to 3 pounds mussels

¼ cup olive oil

1 large onion, grated

4 cloves garlic, finely chopped

1 red bell pepper, chopped

1 cup white wine

2 fresh bay leaves

1 cinnamon stick

1 teaspoon oregano

Salt and pepper

2 tablespoons finely chopped
    fresh parsley

Scrub mussel shells with a hard brush to scrape off any debris and rinse them well with cold water. Heat olive oil in a large pot and sauté the onion, garlic, and red pepper 5 minutes. Add mussels and cook, stirring, 5 more minutes. Add the wine, bay leaves, cinnamon, oregano, and salt and pepper. Sprinkle with chopped parsley, cover, and allow the mixture to cook for 10 to 15 minutes until the mussels open. Serve the mussels hot with their sauce, crusty bread, and wine or ouzo.

♦ *Serves 5 to 6*

Note: Discard any mussels that did not open during cooking.

Mykonos Seafood Triangles

BOUREKAKIA ME KAVOURI KAI GARIDES

S eafood triangles, a real delicacy and easy to prepare, are good hot or cold.

3 tablespoons olive oil

1 large onion, grated

3 cloves garlic, finely chopped

1 pound fresh shrimp, peeled,
   deveined, and chopped

1 cup cleaned lump crabmeat

2 tablespoons chopped fresh parsley

1 tablespoon chopped fresh mint

1 teaspoon paprika

Salt and pepper

1 cup crumbled feta cheese

¼ cup grated kefalotyri or
   Parmesan cheese

1 pound fillo dough

Preheat the oven to 350 degrees. In a large skillet, heat oil over medium-high heat. Add onion and garlic and sauté about 5 minutes. Add shrimp, crabmeat, parsley, mint, paprika, and salt and pepper and stir for 5 minutes. Remove the mixture from the heat, put it in a large bowl, add the feta and kefalotyri cheese, and mix well. Let the mixture chill completely. Prepare the triangles according to the directions on page 201. Bake for 20 to 25 minutes, until golden brown.

◆ *Yields 2½ to 3 dozen*

Olive and Cheese Platter

MEZEDAKI ME ELIES KAI TYRI

This is a delicious appetizer for any party.

1½ cups kalamata olives

1½ cups green cracked olives

1 pound kefalotyri cheese or any
   hard yellow cheese, cut into
   large cubes

1 pound kaseri cheese, cut into
   large cubes

¼ cup olive oil

3 cloves garlic, finely chopped

Juice of 1 or 2 lemons

1 teaspoon finely chopped fresh
   thyme

1 teaspoon finely chopped fresh
   rosemary

1 teaspoon dried oregano

Wash the olives in cold water and drain. Place in a medium bowl and add both cheeses. In a small bowl, mix the oil, garlic, lemon juice, thyme, rosemary, and oregano. Pour the marinade over the olives and cheese and toss well. Cover and marinate for 2 hours before serving. Served with crusty bread and ouzo or wine.

◆ *Serves 4*

Potatoes with Garlic Sauce

Skordalia

5 to 6 russet potatoes

4 to 5 cloves garlic, minced

¼ cup white vinegar

Salt and pepper

½ cup olive oil

Peel the potatoes, place them in a pot, add water to cover completely, and boil them until they are tender, about 45 minutes to 1 hour. Remove from the heat and drain. Process the potatoes in a food processor with the garlic, vinegar, and salt and pepper; slowly add the oil to the mixture, whipping until creamy smooth. This delicious sauce is served warm with fish or as a side dish or appetizer.

◆ *Serves 6*

Georgia's Shrimp with Feta in Fillo

GARIDES ME FETA KAI FILLO

This is one of my favorite appetizers, especially for the holidays.

24 large shrimp, peeled and deveined

Juice of 1 lemon

1 tablespoon olive oil

1 teaspoon dried oregano

½ teaspoon chopped fresh rosemary

3 cloves garlic, crushed

½ teaspoon dried mint

Salt and pepper

½ pound hard feta cheese, cut into long strips ½ inch thick

12 thin pieces ham, cut in half lengthwise

1 pound fillo dough

¼ cup olive oil, to brush fillo

Lemon slices, for garnish

Parsley sprigs, for garnish

Preheat the oven to 350 degrees. Wash the peeled and deveined shrimp in cold water and pat dry. Slice each shrimp and spread it open like a butterfly. Place the shrimp in a large bowl and sprinkle with lemon juice, oil, oregano, rosemary, garlic, mint, and salt and pepper. Mix well, cover, and refrigerate for 3 hours. Remove the shrimp from the marinade; stuff each one with 1 strip of feta cheese and wrap it with a ham strip. Take 2 sheets of fillo dough, brush each one with oil, and stack one on top of another. Cut into 1-inch-wide strips and wrap fillo around each stuffed shrimp so that it forms the natural shape of the shrimp. Brush with oil, place on a cookie sheet, and sprinkle with water. Bake for 30 to 35 minutes, or until golden brown. Remove from the oven and let stand for 10 minutes. Serve on a platter and garnish with lemon slices and parsley sprigs.

♦ *Serves 4 to 5*

Shrimp with Garlic

GARIDES SKORDADES MEZES

This is delicious as an appetizer or as a meal on its own.

¼ cup olive oil

4 cloves garlic, chopped

1 to 1½ pounds shrimp, peeled
  and deveined

1 teaspoon dried oregano

½ teaspoon dried thyme

Juice of 1 lemon

2 bay leaves

½ teaspoon paprika

Salt and pepper

1 tablespoon chopped fresh
  parsley, for garnish

In a large skillet, heat the oil and sauté garlic for 1 minute over medium heat. Add the shrimp and cook, stirring, 2 to 3 minutes. Add oregano, thyme, lemon juice, and bay leaves and sprinkle with paprika and salt and pepper to taste. Stir constantly for 10 minutes. Arrange on a platter; pour the remaining cooking juices over the shrimp and sprinkle with parsley. Serve hot with crusty bread.

◆ *Serves 4 to 5*

Toasted Bread Riganato with Tomatoes and Feta

Psomi Orektiko

This is a popular bread appetizer in Greek restaurants.

1 loaf country-style bread, cut into
   1-inch slices
Olive oil, to brush on bread
3 large fresh tomatoes, peeled,
   seeded, and chopped
2 tablespoons olive oil

1 clove garlic, finely chopped
1 teaspoon dried oregano
½ cup small cubes feta cheese
1 tablespoon finely chopped fresh
   flat parsley
Salt and pepper

Preheat the oven to 375 degrees. Place the bread slices on a cookie sheet and brush them with a little olive oil. Toast in the oven until golden brown, then remove. In a medium bowl, combine the tomatoes, oil, garlic, oregano, and salt and pepper and toss well. Top each bread slice with 2 tablespoons of the tomato mixture, then sprinkle with feta cheese and parsley. Serve as an appetizer or with any meal.

♦ *Serves 5 to 6*

Yiayia's Garlic Sauce

SKORDALIA TIS YIAYIA'S

This is my grandmother's delicious skordalia served with fried fish or as an appetizer.

5 slices day-old Italian bread
½ cup walnuts
5 cloves garlic, minced
¼ cup or more olive oil

¼ cup white vinegar
Salt and pepper
Chopped fresh parsley, for garnish
Kalamata olives, for garnish

Cut the crust off the bread, then dip the bread in water and squeeze out the excess. In a food processor, combine the walnuts, bread, and garlic. Purée for 15 to 20 seconds. Slowly add oil and vinegar; mix well. Season with salt and pepper to taste and continue mixing for 2 more minutes, or until the mixture is smooth. If the mixture appears to be too thick, add a little water. Serve the garlic sauce in a bowl, garnished with parsley and olives.

◆ *Serves 4 to 5*

General Food Tips

Broccoli
Broccoli should be firm with dark green leaves and firm stems. Seal it tightly in a plastic bag and refrigerate for no longer than one week.

Cabbage
Cabbage should be a deep green color and firm to the touch. Store it in a plastic bag and refrigerate for no longer than two to three weeks.

Carrots
Carrots should be firm and bright orange in color. Remove their green tops before refrigerating for one to two weeks in a tightly sealed plastic bag.

Cauliflower
Choose a cauliflower with a very white head and green leaves that hug the white florets. Remove the leaves and store the white part in a sealed plastic bag in the refrigerator for one week.

Chicken

Wash chicken thoroughly and remove the fat. When baking a whole chicken, baste it with a mixture of two tablespoons of olive oil and the juice of one lemon (beaten together to combine). This gives you a nice brown color and makes the chicken crisp and flavorful. The trick is to thoroughly bake or roast the chicken and keep the meat moist by basting often.

Garlic

Heads of garlic should be kept in a cool, dry place no longer than about two months.

Lettuce

Romaine or Boston lettuce should be medium to dark green. Store it in a tightly sealed plastic bag no longer than one week.

Olive oil

I use olive oil frequently. Because I strive for more than just flavor and appearance, I like to offer healthful, low-calorie meals whenever possible. The Greek people have used olive oil for many years, even before it became popular with health-conscious people. Greece is known for its groves of olive trees and the many uses for the fruit they bear.

Parsley

Parsley should be dark, springy, and rich green in color. Untie the bunch and trim the bottoms of the stems slightly, then separate the parsley stems and put them, unwashed, in a tightly sealed plastic bag. Refrigerate for up to one week.

Peppers

Several recipes in this book call for green bell peppers, which should be dark green in color and firm. Because they are more fragile than some other vegetables, seal them in a plastic bag and use within a week.

Potatoes

Potatoes should be firm and stored in a cool, semidark room. Properly stored, they should be good for up to one month.

Scallions

Scallions should be dark green in color and refrigerated for no more than one week.

Soups

One of the most nourishing and appetizing light dishes, soups are wholesome eating and a very good way to begin any meal.

Spinach

Spinach, which should be dark green, should be stored, unwashed, in a plastic bag in the refrigerator and used as soon as possible.

Tomatoes

Tomatoes should be firm and red in color. If they are not ripe, put them in a bowl with an apple or inside a closed brown paper bag at room temperature. If they are too ripe, refrigerate and slice them for garnish.

Zucchini

Zucchini, which are best if small to medium in size, should be firm and dark green. Refrigerate them for four to five days. You can usually leave the skins on.

Georgia teaching a cooking class in Boston.

Soups

- Amalia's Beef Stew   36
- Aromatic Lentil Soup   37
- Bean Soup with Leeks   38
- Black-Eyed Bean Soup   39
- Chicken Soup in Egg Lemon Sauce   40
- Chicken Tomato Soup with Fides   41
- Delicious Chickpea Soup   42
- Georgia's Chicken Broth   43
- Grecian Beef Soup with Vegetables   44
- Lemon Chicken Noodle Soup   45
- Lemon White Bean Soup   46
- Olympia Egg and Lemon Chicken Soup   47
- My Mother's Village-Style Veal Soup   48

Amalia's Beef Stew

STIFATHO AMALIADOS

Serve crusty bread with this delicious stew so you can dunk it into the sauce.

3 to 3½ pounds beef stew chunks	2 bay leaves
½ cup olive oil	8 peppercorns
½ cup red wine	Salt and pepper
1½ cups crushed plum tomatoes	2½ to 3 cups water
1½ tablespoons tomato paste	1 to 1½ pounds small whole
½ teaspoon sugar	white onions
6 cloves garlic, peeled	¼ cup olive oil, for frying onion
1 cinnamon stick	3 tablespoons wine vinegar
3 whole cloves	

Wash the meat and pat dry. Heat ¼ cup of the oil in a large pot and sauté the meat until light brown. Add wine and stir to combine. Add tomatoes, tomato paste, sugar, garlic, cinnamon, cloves, bay leaves, peppercorns, and salt and pepper; then add the water, cover, and simmer for 1½ hours. Peel the onions, then wash them and pat dry. In a large skillet, heat the remaining ¼ cup of oil and lightly fry the onions. Remove onions from the skillet with a slotted spoon and add them to the pot with the meat. Stir in vinegar and more water, if needed, and cook for 25 to 30 more minutes, until meat and onions are cooked. Remove whole cloves, cinnamon, bay leaves, and peppercorns before serving.

◆ *Serves 6*

Aromatic Lentil Soup

AROMATIKI FAKI SOUPA

Lentil soup is my brother (Taki) Peter's favorite. This soup, a meal in itself, is great on cold, wintry days. It can be served alone or with kalamata olives, bread, and any table cheese you like.

1 pound dried brown lentils	2 bay leaves
¼ cup olive oil	½ teaspoon dried oregano
1 cup finely chopped onion	1 cinnamon stick
4 cloves garlic, finely chopped	¼ teaspoon allspice
2 cups peeled and finely chopped	½ teaspoon dried mint
fresh tomatoes, with juice	3 tablespoons red wine vinegar
1 tablespoon tomato paste	Salt and pepper

Wash and sort the lentils, put in a large pot, cover with water, and bring to a boil. Cook for 15 minutes, remove from the heat, and drain all the liquid. Return the lentils to the pot and add fresh water to cover—2½ to 3 quarts. Half-cover the pot and simmer for 30 minutes. Stir in oil, onions, garlic, tomatoes, tomato paste, bay leaves, oregano, cinnamon, allspice, and mint; cover and cook 1 hour or more. Add vinegar and salt and pepper to taste. Remove from the heat, let stand for 5 minutes, and serve hot.

◆ *Serves 6*

Bean Soup with Leeks

FASOLIA ME PRASA

Serve this delicious soup with crusty bread and kalamata olives on the side.

1 pound dried cannellini (white kidney) beans	3 cloves garlic, sliced
	1½ cups canned crushed tomatoes
¼ cup olive oil	1 tablespoon tomato paste
1 medium onion, chopped	Salt and pepper
2 cups chopped leeks	Juice of 1 lemon (optional)
2 carrots, chopped	2 tablespoons chopped fresh
2 celery stalks, with leaves, sliced	parsley, for garnish

Place the beans in a large bowl and fill with enough water to cover. Soak for 8 hours or overnight, rinse, and drain. Put beans in a large pot and add enough water to completely cover them; boil for 20 minutes. Drain the liquid and return the beans to the pot; add 3 to 3½ quarts of water and boil, half-covered, for 1 hour. Add oil, onion, leeks, carrots, celery, garlic, crushed tomatoes, and tomato paste. Add more water if needed. Cover and simmer for 45 to 50 minutes, or until beans are tender. Season with salt and pepper. To serve, sprinkle on some fresh lemon juice (optional) and garnish with chopped parsley. Serve with crusty bread.

◆ *Serves 6*

Black-Eyed Bean Soup

Mavromatika Fasolia Soupa

This wonderful soup can be served with crusty bread, kalamata olives, and a glass of good wine.

1 pound dried black-eyed beans

¼ cup olive oil

1 large onion, chopped

3 cloves garlic, chopped

1½ cups canned crushed tomatoes

2 leeks, chopped, white part only

1 large carrot, chopped

½ cup chopped celery

2 tablespoons chopped fresh dill

2 bay leaves

Salt and pepper

Place the beans in a large pot with enough water to cover. Bring to a boil over high heat, cook for 15 minutes, then drain. Return the beans to the pot, add enough water to cover, and add the remaining ingredients. Bring to a boil over medium heat and cook for 1 hour, or until beans are tender. You may need to add water to keep the soup at the desired consistency.

◆ *Serves 5 to 6*

Chicken Soup in Egg Lemon Sauce

Yiouvarelakia me Kota Avgolemono

This soup is delicious, light, and healthy. I love it!

1½ pounds ground chicken breast	1 tablespoon finely chopped
½ cup uncooked long-grain	fresh mint
white rice	1 egg, lightly beaten
1 large onion, grated and drained	8 cups chicken broth
1 tablespoon finely chopped	2 tablespoons olive oil
fresh parsley	Salt and pepper

In a large bowl, combine ground chicken, rice, onion, parsley, mint, and egg. Knead until the ingredients are mixed well. Into a medium saucepan, add chicken broth, olive oil, and salt and pepper to taste. Bring to a boil and cook for 10 minutes. Shape the chicken mixture into small balls and add them to the pot. Reduce heat to medium and continue cooking for 30 to 40 minutes, or until the chicken and rice are tender, adding water if necessary.

Egg lemon sauce:

2 eggs	Juice of 1 to 2 lemons

To make the sauce, beat 2 eggs in a blender and add lemon juice. While beating the sauce, slowly add 1 cup of hot broth from the pot to the egg mixture, then pour the egg mixture back into the pot. Simmer over low heat until the broth thickens, being very careful not to allow it to come to a boil. Serve hot.

♦ *Serves 5 to 6*

Chicken Tomato Soup with Fides

Ntomatosoupa me Fides

My mother would make this soup for a light lunch or dinner.

7 cups chicken broth

1 can (28 ounces) crushed tomatoes

2 tablespoons olive oil

1½ cups Greek fides pasta or fine
  egg noodles

Salt and pepper

½ cup freshly grated Parmesan
  cheese, for garnish

2 tablespoons chopped fresh
  parsley, for garnish

Into a medium pot, add broth, crushed tomatoes, and olive oil; bring to a boil and simmer 20 minutes. Stir in fides or noodles and salt and pepper and cook over medium heat for 10 to 12 minutes. Garnish the top of the soup with the grated cheese and chopped parsley and serve hot.

◆ *Serves 5 to 6*

Note: Fides pasta (similar to fine egg noodles) is available in Greek markets.

Delicious Chickpea Soup

Revithia Soupa

Serve this healthy soup with kalamata olives and crusty bread.

1 pound dried chickpeas

1 tablespoon baking soda

¼ cup olive oil

1 cup chopped onions

3 cloves garlic, chopped

½ cup chopped celery

1 pound ripe tomatoes, peeled and
    crushed, with juice

2 teaspoons tomato paste

1 bay leaf

Salt and pepper

Wash the chickpeas in cold water and soak them overnight. Drain, sprinkle with the baking soda, and let stand for 25 minutes. Remove the chickpeas' skin by rubbing them between your thumb and forefinger. Rinse well with cold water and drain. In large saucepan, heat oil and sauté onion, garlic, and celery for 5 minutes. Add chickpeas, crushed tomatoes, tomato paste, and enough water to cover (about 10 cups). Cover, bring to a boil, and cook over medium heat for 1½ hours, or until the chickpeas are tender. Stir occasionally, adding salt and pepper and more water if needed. Remove from heat and serve hot.

◆ *Serves 6*

Georgia's Chicken Broth

Kotozoumo

1 chicken (3 to 3½ pounds)	1 large carrot, cut up
1½ teaspoons salt	1 onion, cut up
½ teaspoon pepper	1 bay leaf
1 celery stalk with leaves, cut up	2 sprigs parsley

Remove skin and any excess fat from the chicken. Place chicken in a large pot with enough water to cover. Add remaining ingredients and bring to a boil. Skim any foam off the broth and reduce heat to medium. Cover and simmer for about 1½ hours, or until the chicken is cooked. Remove chicken from the pot and reserve. Allow broth to cool slightly, then strain it through cheesecloth. Discard the vegetables; bone the chicken and cut the meat into pieces. Cover and refrigerate the broth and chicken in separate containers no more than 2 days, or freeze the broth for no more than 3 months.

◆ *Yields 4 to 4½ cups*

Grecian Beef Soup with Vegetables

Mosxari Soupa me Horta

Served hot with crusty bread, this hearty soup is delicious as a main course.

2½ to 3 pounds beef or veal chunks

¼ cup olive oil

1 large onion, chopped

1 cup thinly sliced celery

3 cloves garlic, minced

1½ cups canned whole tomatoes, chopped, with juice

1 tablespoon tomato paste

8 to 10 cups water

½ teaspoon dried oregano

2 bay leaves

1 cinnamon stick

1 cup sliced carrots

2 cups peeled and cubed russet potatoes (1-inch cubes)

1 cup frozen peas

1 can (14 ounces) artichoke hearts, drained and cut in half

Salt and pepper

Wash meat and pat dry. In a large, heavy skillet, heat oil and sauté meat until browned on all sides. Remove meat with a slotted spoon and transfer to a large soup pot. To the skillet, add onion, celery, and garlic and sauté for 5 minutes, or until soft. Transfer the mixture to the pot with the meat, add tomatoes, tomato paste, water, oregano, bay leaves, and cinnamon and bring the mixture to a boil. Lower the heat, cover, and simmer for 1½ hours, or until meat is tender. Add potatoes and carrots and cook for another 30 minutes. Add peas, artichoke hearts, and salt and pepper and cook for 15 minutes more, until meat and vegetables are tender. Add more water during cooking if necessary. Remove from the stove and let stand for 5 minutes. Serve hot.

◆ *Serves 6*

Lemon Chicken Noodle Soup

KOTA SOUPA ME XILOPITES

Prepare this soup with Georgia's chicken broth. The results are delicious.

5 cups chicken broth

2 to 3 cups water

1 tablespoon olive oil

1 cup sliced carrots

1 cup sliced celery

½ cup chopped onion

1 bay leaf

1½ cups uncooked soup noodles

Reserved cut-up chicken

½ cup frozen peas

Salt and pepper

Juice of 1 lemon

1 tablespoon chopped fresh parsley

Into a large pot, add broth, water, oil, carrots, celery, onion, bay leaf. Bring to a boil, reduce heat, and simmer, covered, for 25 minutes, or until the vegetables are tender. Add noodles, cut-up chicken and frozen peas, and stir. Add salt and pepper and cook, uncovered, for 20 minutes, or until the noodles are tender. Add lemon juice and cook for 1 to 2 minutes more. Remove from heat and serve hot, sprinkled with parsley.

◆ *Serves 5 to 6*

Note: To prepare chicken broth, see page 43.

Lemon White Bean Soup

FASOLATHA ME LEMON

This healthy soup is my mother's recipe. It can be served with kalamata olives, crusty bread, and a glass of wine.

1 pound dried cannellini
   (white kidney) beans
¼ cup olive oil
1 large onion, finely chopped
2 cloves garlic, chopped

1 cup sliced carrots
1 cup thinly sliced celery
1 bay leaf
Salt and pepper
Juice of 2 lemons

Sort and wash the beans, place in a large bowl with enough water to cover, and soak overnight. Rinse and drain, put in a large pot with enough water to cover, and bring to a boil. Cook for 30 minutes, then remove from the stove and drain. Return beans to the pot, add enough water to cover, and bring to a boil. Cook for 1 hour. Add oil, onion, garlic, carrots, celery, bay leaf, and salt and pepper and cook over medium heat for 1 more hour, or until beans are tender, adding more water if necessary. Turn off heat and stir in lemon juice. Serve hot.

♦ *Serves 6*

Olympia Egg and Lemon Chicken Soup

KOTOSOUPA AVGOLEMONONO

Greek cuisine is known for its egg and lemon chicken soup. The rich egg and lemon sauce gives the soup a taste that makes it a meal by itself. Serve it with chicken pieces, crusty bread, and a glass of wine. Try it and you'll love it!

1 whole chicken (3 to 3½ pounds)	Salt
2 small onions, peeled	¾ cup uncooked orzo pasta or
1 medium carrot, peeled and cut	white long-grain rice
into 3 pieces	Salt and pepper
1 celery stalk, cut into 3 pieces	2 eggs, at room temperature
1 tablespoon olive oil	Juice of 2 lemons

Remove the skin and fat from the chicken; rinse and drain. Place whole chicken into a large pot with enough water to cover; add onions, carrot, celery, olive oil, and salt. Bring to a boil, skimming off the foam frequently. Cook, half-covered, for 1½ hours, or until the chicken meat comes away from the bones. Remove pot from the heat and, with a slotted spoon, remove chicken, onions, celery, and carrots from the pot; reserve. Add more broth or water to keep the soup at the desired consistency. Strain the chicken broth with cheesecloth and return it to the pot. Bring the pot to a boil, add orzo or rice, and stir well. Simmer, uncovered, for 25 to 30 minutes and add more salt and pepper to taste. Bone chicken meat, cut into chunks, and add to the pot. Blend the eggs and add the lemon juice, beating continuously. Slowly add 1 cup of hot chicken broth to the egg lemon mixture while continuing to beat. Add the egg lemon broth mixture to the pot, stirring constantly. Cook over low heat for 1 to 2 minutes, but do not allow the soup to come to a boil. Remove from the heat and serve hot.

◆ *Serves 6*

My Mother's Village-Style Veal Soup

HORIATIKI SOUPA

My mother made this soup all the time, and I loved it!

3 to 3½ pounds veal stew chunks

¼ cup olive oil

3 cloves garlic, chopped

½ cup red wine

1½ cups canned crushed tomatoes

8 small gourmet whole potatoes, peeled

2 medium carrots, peeled and cut into 1-inch rounds

6 to 8 small white onions, peeled

3 stalks of celery, sliced

2 to 3 small zucchini, cut into 1½- to 2-inch rounds

1 tablespoon chopped fresh dill

1 tablespoon chopped fresh parsley

Salt and pepper

Juice of 1 to 2 lemons

Wash and pat the meat dry. In a large stewing pot, heat oil, then add meat and brown on all sides. Add enough water to reach the middle of the pot, cover, and bring to a boil. Reduce the heat to medium and cook for 1½ hours, or until the meat is almost tender. Add garlic, red wine, crushed tomatoes, potatoes, carrots, onions, celery, zucchini, dill, parsley, and salt and pepper; add more water if necessary, and cook until the vegetables and meat are tender. Add lemon juice 10 minutes before the soup is ready. Remove from the heat and serve hot with toasted crusty bread.

◆ *Serves 6*

GREEK HERBS AND SPICES

A dd herbs in small amounts, one-quarter of a teaspoon for each four servings, and taste before adding more. Crush dried herbs or snip fresh ones just before using them. If you are substituting fresh for dried, use three times more fresh herbs.

Basil
Basil is aromatic and has a sweet, warm flavor, whether used whole or ground. It is good with lamb, fish, roasts, stews, ground beef, vegetables, dressings, and omelets.

Bay leaves
Bay leaves have a pungent flavor. Use the whole leaf but remove it before serving. They are good in vegetable dishes, fish and seafood, stews, and pickles.

Cinnamon
Virtually all of the cinnamon sold in the United States is the full-bodied, pungent cassia variety.

Cloves

Famous for their spicy fragrance, these nail-shaped buds are imported from Madagascar and Zanzibar.

Coriander

One of the first herbs known to mankind, coriander is grown in Morocco, Europe, and South America.

Dill

Both the seeds and the leaves of dill are flavorful. Leaves may be used as a garnish with fish, soup, dressings, potatoes, and beans. Leaves or the whole flat may be used to make dilled pickles.

Garlic

Formerly used to ward off evil spirits, flavorful garlic is used widely in French and Italian cooking. Greek chefs use it mostly in roasts and sauces.

Honey

Nectar from the flowers, worked and delivered through bees, honey is often used in place of granulated sugar. This thick and sweet syrup has many uses.

Mint

Mint leaves, aromatic with a cool flavor, are excellent in beverages, with fish, cheese, lamb, soup, peas, and carrots, and in fruit desserts.

Nutmeg
Once sold as a charm, nutmeg has a warm and spicy flavor. It is tropical in origin.

Olive oil
Oil from olives imparts a delicate, delicious flavor to foods and makes them easier to digest and better for us.

Oregano
Use oregano, with its strong aromatic odor, whole or ground to spice tomato juice, fish, eggs, pizza, omelets, chili, stew, gravy, poultry, and vegetables.

Parsley
Parsley is best when used fresh, but it can be used dry as well. Use it as a garnish or for seasoning with fish, omelets, soups, meats, stuffing, and mixed greens.

Rosemary
Very aromatic, rosemary can be used fresh or dried to season fish, stuffing, beef, lamb, poultry, onions, eggs, and bread.

Saffron
Orange-yellow in color, saffron is used to flavor or color foods. Use it in soup, chicken, rice, and fancy breads.

Sage

Sage may be used fresh or dried, and the flowers are sometimes used in salads. Add to tomato juice, fish, fondue, omelets, beef, poultry, stuffing, cheese, spreads, cornbread, and biscuits.

Thyme

This slightly pungent herb, one of the most popular, is grown mainly in France and Spain.

Georgia and her son Peter.

Salads

- Bean Salad   54
- Beet Salad   55
- Boiled Cauliflower Salad   56
- Chickpea Salad   57
- Potato and Artichoke Salad   58
- Potato and Chicken Salad   59
- Romaine Lettuce Salad   60
- Tomato and Cucumber Salad   61
- Zucchini Salad   62

Bean Salad

FASOLIA SALATA

1 pound cannellini (white kidney)
   beans
1 medium red onion, chopped
1 small red bell pepper, chopped
¼ cup finely chopped fresh parsley
¼ cup olive oil
Juice of 1½ lemons
2 cloves garlic, minced

½ teaspoon dried oregano
Salt and pepper
1 small red onion, sliced, for
   garnish
1 medium tomato, sliced, for
   garnish
10 kalamata olives, for garnish

Soak and boil the beans according to package directions. Remove from the heat, drain the beans in a colander, and cool. Place beans in a large bowl and add the onion, red pepper, and parsley. In a small jar, shake the oil, lemon juice, garlic, oregano, and salt and pepper. Pour over the salad and toss well. Garnish the salad with onion and tomato slices and olives. Serve this salad as a side dish.

♦ *Serves 4 to 5*

Beet Salad

Patzarosalata

I like to serve this delicious salad with any dish, especially with fish.

2½ to 3 pounds fresh beets
Salt
¼ cup olive oil

4 cloves garlic, minced
2 to 3 tablespoons wine vinegar

Cut the green leaves off the beets and slice leaves into 1½-inch pieces. Place them in a colander and rinse 3 or 4 times with cold water. Wash and scrub the roots thoroughly. In a large saucepan, add roots and enough cold water to cover. Bring to a boil, add salt, and cook for 35 minutes. Add leaves and cook 10 more minutes, or until tender. Remove from the heat, drain the water, and cool. Cut beets into quarters and garnish with the green leaves. In a small bowl, mix olive oil, garlic, and vinegar well and pour the dressing over the salad. Serve cold or at room temperature.

◆ *Serves 4*

Boiled Cauliflower Salad

KOUNOUPITHI SALATA

1 large cauliflower (2½ to 3 pounds)
Salt
¼ cup olive oil
Juice of 1 to 2 fresh lemons

1 tablespoon chopped fresh flat
   parsley
6 to 8 kalamata olives, for garnish

Cut off the cauliflower's outer leaves and stem, then cut the head into large pieces, wash, and drain. In a large pot, bring to boil enough water to cover the cauliflower. Add the cauliflower and salt, return to a boil, and cook for 25 to 30 minutes, or until tender. Remove from the pot, drain, and place in a salad bowl. Drizzle the top with olive oil and lemon juice, sprinkle with parsley, and garnish with olives. Serve warm or cold.

◆ *Serves 4*

Chickpea Salad

REVITHOSALATA

This delicious salad can be served alone for a light lunch or dinner.

2 (14-ounce) cans chickpeas
1 can (14 ounces) artichoke hearts
1 medium red onion, sliced
2 medium tomatoes, peeled, seeded, and chopped

1 small cucumber, diced
1 small green bell pepper, chopped
1 tablespoon chopped fresh parsley
½ cup diced feta cheese
10 to 12 kalamata olives

Drain the chickpea liquid, rinse in a colander with cold water, and drain well. Drain the artichokes and slice them in half. In a large salad bowl, combine chickpeas, artichoke hearts, onion, tomatoes, cucumber, green pepper, and parsley. Top with feta cheese and olives.

Dressing:

¼ cup olive oil
Juice of 1 lemon
2 cloves garlic, minced

½ teaspoon dried oregano
Salt and pepper

For the dressing, combine oil, lemon juice, garlic, oregano, and salt and pepper in a small jar and shake well. Pour dressing over the salad and toss well. Serve at room temperature or cold with pita bread.

◆ Serves 4 to 5

Potato and Artichoke Salad

PATATOSALATA ME AGINARES

This is a perfect light meal with crusty bread and wine.

2 to 2½ pounds small new potatoes, unpeeled

2 (14-ounce) cans artichoke hearts, drained and cut in half

1 small red onion, chopped

¼ cup chopped scallions

1 tablespoon finely chopped fresh parsley

1 tablespoon finely chopped fresh dill

12 kalamata olives

Wash potatoes (do not peel them), place them in a large saucepan with enough cool water to cover, and bring them to a boil. Cook for 45 minutes, or until tender. Remove from heat, drain, and allow potatoes cool. Peel them and place them in a large salad bowl. Add artichokes to the potatoes and top with onion, scallions, parsley, dill, and olives.

Dressing:

¼ cup olive oil

2 to 3 tablespoons wine vinegar or juice of 1 lemon

1 teaspoon dried oregano

½ teaspoon dried thyme

Salt and pepper

To prepare the dressing, combine olive oil, vinegar or lemon juice, oregano, thyme, and salt and pepper in a small jar and shake well. Pour the dressing on the salad and toss. Serve at room temperature.

◆ *Serves 4 to 5*

Potato and Chicken Salad

Salata me Patates kai Kota

This delicious salad is great for lunch or dinner with pita bread.

2 cups cooked and cubed chicken
    breasts
2 cups cooked and cubed potatoes
2 medium tomatoes, skinned and
    cut into cubes
1 cucumber, peeled and cut
    into cubes

1 small red onion, chopped
1 small green bell pepper, chopped
1½ tablespoons chopped fresh flat
    parsley
10 kalamata olives, for garnish

In a large salad bowl, combine chicken, potatoes, tomatoes, cucumber, onion, green pepper, and parsley and toss.

Dressing:

¼ cup olive oil
3 tablespoons red wine vinegar
½ teaspoon dried thyme

½ teaspoon dried oregano
1 clove garlic, crushed
Salt and pepper

To make the dressing, mix oil, vinegar, thyme, oregano, garlic, and salt and pepper to taste in a small jar. Pour over the salad and garnish with olives.

◆ Serves 4

Romaine Lettuce Salad

MAROULOSALATA

This salad is especially made for Greek Easter. Serve with roasted lamb.

1 large head romaine lettuce,
   thinly sliced
½ cup chopped scallions

2 tablespoons finely chopped
   fresh dill

Place lettuce in a large bowl and add scallions and dill.

Dressing:

¼ cup olive oil
Juice of 1 lemon

½ teaspoon dried oregano
Salt

To prepare the dressing, combine the oil, lemon juice, oregano, and salt to taste in a small jar. Shake well, pour over the salad, and toss well.

◆ *Serves 4*

Tomato and Cucumber Salad

Salata me Agouri kai Tomata

For this delicious salad, the only dressing used is olive oil.

4 ripe tomatoes, cut into wedges

2 medium cucumbers, sliced

1 small red onion, sliced

10 to 15 kalamata olives

¼ cup olive oil

1 teaspoon dried oregano

Salt and pepper to taste

½ cup cubed feta cheese

In a large salad bowl, combine tomatoes, cucumbers, onion, and olives. Add olive oil and season with oregano and salt and pepper. Top with feta cheese and toss gently. Served with crusty bread, this salad is delicious for lunch or dinner.

♦ *Serves 4*

Zucchini Salad

KOLOKITHAKIA SALATA

This wonderful salad is very light and will impress your family.

1½ to 2 pounds small zucchini

Wash the zucchini well and cut off stems. Place in a large pot with enough water to cover and bring to a boil. Cook for 25 to 30 minutes or until tender. Remove zucchini from the pot, drain, and slice into 1½-inch-long pieces.

Dressing:

¼ cup olive oil

2 to 3 tablespoons wine vinegar

½ teaspoon oregano

3 cloves garlic, minced

Salt and pepper

Fresh parsley, for garnish

To prepare the dressing, combine the oil, vinegar, oregano, garlic, and salt and pepper in a jar and shake well. Pour dressing over zucchini, but do not toss. Garnish with parsley and serve cold or at room temperature.

◆ *Serves 4*

GREEK OLIVES

Greece is world famous for its olives, used for eating and cooking. They come in a number of varieties, colors, and sizes. The following types of olives are easy to find in U.S. markets.

Kalamata black olives

These olives are almond shaped and have a distinctive flavor from the vinegar used in the curing process. The best ones are meaty and firm after curing for five to six months. Named after the city of Kalamatas in the southwest of Peloponnese, these olives are delicious used as appetizers, in salads, or for cooking.

Amfissa olives

These olives are grown and produced in northwest Athens. Round and black, with a pleasantly sweet and nutty flavor, they are great for making olive dip or as an appetizer sprinkled with lemon, olive oil, and oregano and served with crusty bread.

Cracked green olives

These delicious olives are grown and produced throughout the countryside of Greece. They are small or large depending on whether they are harvested before their color changes from light or from dark green. They have a strong, sharp flavor and are delicious marinated with olive oil, vinegar or lemon juice, oregano, garlic, and fresh thyme. Serve them as an appetizer with cheese, crusty bread, and ouzo.

Hondroelia giant olives

These large olives are round and greenish purple. Meaty and flavorful, they can be served from their brine and are delicious sprinkled with olive oil, lemon juice, and oregano.

Elitses

These olives are very small, with a sweet flavor. They are harvested mostly around the island of Crete.

A variety of Greek olives. Photo courtesy of Morea Olives.

Dressings and Sauces

- A Touch of Georgia's Dressing   66
- Aromatic Marinade   67
- Georgia-Style Béchamel Sauce   68
- Margarita's Tomato Sauce   69
- Oil, Lemon, and Garlic Dressing   70
- Ouzo Marinade for Grilled Steaks   71
- Rosemary Marinade   72
- Wine Marinade for Beef or Lamb Kabobs   73

A Touch of Georgia's Dressing

Lathoxitho

½ cup olive oil

¼ cup wine vinegar

1 tablespoon finely chopped fresh
   oregano

2 cloves garlic, finely chopped

½ teaspoon dried basil

½ teaspoon crushed red pepper
   (optional)

Salt and freshly ground pepper

In a medium bowl, combine ingredients and blend very well with a fork
or whisk until the sauce thickens. Served with any fresh salad or grilled
vegetables.

♦ *Yields ¾ cup*

Aromatic Marinade

AROMATIKI MARINARA

This aromatic marinade is used for grilled fish.

½ cup olive oil

Juice of 2 lemons

2 tablespoons finely chopped
  fresh basil

1 tablespoon finely chopped fresh
  oregano

1 tablespoon finely chopped
  fresh thyme

3 cloves garlic, minced

Salt and pepper

In a medium bowl, mix all ingredients well. Use this sauce to marinate shrimp, swordfish, tuna, or halibut steaks for 3 hours in the refrigerator before cooking.

◆ Yields ¾ cup

Georgia-Style Béchamel Sauce

BÉCHAMEL

This béchamel sauce is used for moussaka or pastitsio.

½ cup (1 stick) butter
¾ cup flour
5 cups hot milk
2 egg yolks

Salt and white pepper
3 tablespoons grated kefalotyri or
    Parmesan cheese
½ teaspoon nutmeg

In a large saucepan over medium heat, melt the butter and gradually add the flour, stirring continuously for 2 to 3 minutes. Add the hot milk and keep stirring until it reaches a smooth and creamy consistency. Remove the saucepan from the heat. In a medium bowl, beat the egg yolks and slowly add 1½ cups of the hot mixture to the eggs and beat well. Return egg mixture to the saucepan and add salt and pepper, cheese, and nutmeg, stirring constantly. Simmer until the mixture is thick and smooth.

◆ *Yields 4 to 4½ cups*

Note: This is the correct amount of béchamel sauce for a moussaka (see page 156) or pastitsio (see page 138).

Margarita's Tomato Sauce

Saltsa me Tomata

This is my mother's special sauce; the cinnamon and clove flavors always make my mouth water. This is great over pasta or meatballs, or with braised meats, beef, veal, or lamb.

¼ cup olive oil

1 large onion, grated

3 cloves garlic, minced

2 (14-ounce) cans crushed tomatoes

1 tablespoon tomato paste

¼ cup white wine

2 small cinnamon sticks

2 whole cloves

1 bay leaf

1 teaspoon sugar

Salt and pepper

1 cup water

In a large saucepan, heat oil, then add onion and sauté 2 to 3 minutes. Add garlic and sauté for 1 minute. Add tomatoes, tomato paste, and wine, stirring with a wooden spoon. Add the cinnamon, cloves, bay leaf, sugar, and salt and pepper. Add the water and stir for 2 minutes, then lower the heat and allow the sauce to simmer for 35 to 40 minutes, stirring often but gently, until the sauce thickened. Serve hot.

◆ *Serves 4 to 5*

Oil, Lemon, and Garlic Dressing

LATHOLEMONO SKORDATO

½ cup olive oil

Juice of 2 lemons

3 cloves garlic, minced

1 teaspoon dried oregano

½ teaspoon dried thyme

Salt and freshly ground pepper

Combine ingredients in a medium bowl and blend well with a fork or whisk until the sauce thickens. Pour over salads, grilled fish, or shellfish.

♦ *Yields about ¾ cup*

Note: For vegetables or salads, you can replace the lemon juice with red wine vinegar.

Ouzo Marinade for Grilled Steaks

Ouzo Marinara

½ cup olive oil

3 tablespoons ouzo

Juice of 2 lemons

1 teaspoon grated lemon zest

4 cloves garlic, minced

1 tablespoon finely chopped fresh
oregano

1 teaspoon finely chopped fresh
rosemary

1 bay leaf, crushed

Salt and freshly ground pepper

Combine ingredients and mix well. Marinate steaks in the refrigerator for
at least 6 hours or overnight before cooking.

◆ *Yields ¾ to 1 cup*

Rosemary Marinade

Detrolivano Marinara

This marinade is great for grilled chicken or pork chops.

½ cup lemon juice

1 teaspoon lemon zest

2 teaspoons honey

2 cloves garlic, minced

3 tablespoons olive oil

2 teaspoons chopped fresh
   rosemary leaves

½ teaspoon dried oregano

Salt and pepper

In a small bowl, combine ingredients and mix well. Pour over chicken or pork and marinate for a few hours before cooking.

◆ *Yields ¾ cup*

Wine Marinade for Beef or Lamb Kabobs

MARINARA ME KRASI

1½ cups dry red wine
¼ cup olive oil
4 cloves garlic, crushed
2 tablespoons chopped fresh
    oregano

1 teaspoon finely chopped fresh
    rosemary
1 bay leaf, crushed
Salt and freshly ground pepper

Combine ingredients and mix well. Marinate meat for 8 to 12 hours in the refrigerator, turning occasionally.

◆ *Yields about 1¾ cups*

Note: This can also be used to marinate a whole leg of lamb.

GREEK CHEESES

Cheese is part of the table in every Greek home. The right cheese is a wonderful addition to any meal, from the simplest to the most complex. Cheese can be served before the main course as a meze (appetizer); a platter of different cheeses and wine can be a great starting point to a great dinner. The best-known Greek cheeses are:

Feta
Feta, the most famous and tastiest ancient Greek cheese, is made from sheep's milk in round or square pieces, which are stored in wooden barrels or tin cans. Feta is a white cheese and can be either soft or hard. Serve it as an appetizer (meze) with ouzo, on top of salads, to make savory pies, and as part of many different dishes.

Kefalotyri
Kefalotyri is a hard yellow cheese made from a combination of sheep's and goat milk. Well salted and with a strong, sharp flavor, it can be eaten as an appetizer (meze), grated on pasta or main dishes, or grilled.

Mizithra

Mizithra, which can be either soft or hard cheese, is very similar to mounouri and is made from a number of different types of milk. Soft mizithra is used as a table cheese or to make sweet or savory pies, and hard mizithra is used for grating.

Kaseri

Kaseri is a delicious table cheese made from sheep's milk. It has a sharp flavor and aroma and is excellent for grilling or dicing or in sandwiches.

Anthotiro

Anthotiro is like soft mizithra and similar to ricotta. It is used for sweet or savory pies and spreads.

Kefalograviera

Kefalograviera, a hard yellow cheese, is made from cow's milk. Different regions of Greece make it with sheep's milk, which creates a slightly sharp flavor. It is delicious as an appetizer (meze) or grated.

Haloumi

Haloumi, from Cyprus, is a white cheese made from goat's milk. It is used for grilling and for saganaki.

Gruyère

Gruyère is a hard yellow cheese very similar to kefalograviera. It is made from cow's milk mixed with sheep's milk. With its sweet flavor, Gruyère is great as an appetizer (meze) or grated.

A street vendor in Peloponnese, Greece.

Vegetarian Dishes

- Baked Lima Butter Beans   81
- Baked Potatoes with Onions   82
- Cauliflower Stew with Onions   83
- Eggplant Ragout   84
- Fried Eggplant with Tomato Sauce   85
- Green Beans with Zucchini   87
- Lemon Fava Beans with Artichokes   88
- Lemon Roast Potatoes   89
- Meatless Stuffed Peppers and Tomatoes with Rice   90
- Potatoes Yiahni   92
- Rice with Spinach and Lemon   93
- String Beans with Potatoes   94
- Stuffed Zucchini with Rice   95
- Vegetarian Stuffed Cabbage with Egg and Lemon Sauce   96
- Vegetarian Stuffed Grape Leaves with Rice   98
- Zucchini Ragout   99

The essential ingredients for traditional Greek vegetarian dishes are seasonal vegetables, greens, herbs, and grains. The roots of many of these dishes lie in Greek's rich history and traditions.

The Greek word for vegetarian dishes is ladera, cooked with olive oil, because olive oil is their main condiment. Ladera can be prepared with fresh green beans, artichokes, green peas, okra, zucchini, and tomato sauce. Herbs for ladera include fresh flat parsley, dill, mint, basil, thyme, bay leaves, oregano, rosemary, coriander, fennel, and sage. Ladera are served as complete meals, accompanied with feta cheese and country bread. This chapter covers the traditional vegetarian dishes that my mother made in her kitchen and that my daughter and I make in our kitchens today.

Georgia's daughter, Daisy.

Baked Lima Butter Beans

FASOLIA GIGANDES

This dish is inexpensive and high in protein, despite its lack of meat.

1 pound dried Greek giant beans
    or lima beans
¼ cup olive oil
1 large onion, finely chopped
3 cloves garlic, thinly sliced
2 medium carrots, sliced
3 large tomatoes, peeled and
    chopped, with the juice

1 tablespoon tomato paste
2 cups water
1 teaspoon sugar
Salt and pepper
2 tablespoons finely chopped fresh
    flat parsley

Preheat the oven to 350 degrees. Wash the beans well, discarding any little stones, and soak overnight. Drain and put them in a large pan with enough water to cover. Bring to a boil and cook for 1 hour. Remove beans from the heat and drain again. Heat oil in a saucepan and add onion, garlic, and carrots. Sauté for 5 minutes. Add tomatoes, tomato paste, 1 cup of the water, sugar, salt and pepper, and parsley. Cover and allow to simmer for 20 minutes. Place drained beans in a baking pan, pour the tomato sauce over them, and mix. Add 1 cup water and bake for about 45 minutes to 1 hour, or until they are done and the liquid has been absorbed. Remove from the oven, let stand 10 minutes, and serve.

♦ *Serves 6*

Baked Potatoes with Onions

Patates Psites me Kremidia

6 to 7 medium potatoes, baked,
   peeled, and quartered

1 large onion, thinly sliced

4 cloves garlic, sliced

2 tablespoons chopped fresh mint

2 tomatoes, peeled and chopped

1 teaspoon dried oregano

½ teaspoon dried thyme

Salt and pepper

¼ cup olive oil

1 cup water

1 teaspoon paprika

Preheat the oven to 350 degrees. Wash and drain potatoes and place them in a large bowl. Add onion, garlic, mint, tomatoes, oregano, thyme, and salt and pepper and mix well with your hands. Place the mixture in a baking pan and drizzle with olive oil. Add 1 cup water and sprinkle with paprika. Bake for 1½ hours, or until the potatoes are tender and golden brown.

♦ *Serves 6*

Cauliflower Stew with Onions

KOUNOUPITHI STIFATHO

This is a delicious vegetarian dish.

2½ to 3 pounds cauliflower

¼ cup olive oil

7 to 8 small white onions, peeled

3 cloves garlic, sliced

1½ cups peeled and crushed fresh
   tomatoes or canned crushed
   tomatoes

1½ teaspoons tomato paste

1 cinnamon stick

2 bay leaves

1 small sprig fresh rosemary

Salt and pepper

1 tablespoon vinegar

1 cup water

Clean cauliflower and cut into large pieces. Rinse with cold water and pat dry. In a large pot, heat olive oil, then add cauliflower and sauté until lightly brown. Remove from the pot and set aside. Add onions and garlic to the pot and sauté 5 minutes. Add tomatoes, tomato paste, cinnamon, bay leaves, rosemary, salt and pepper, and vinegar. Add 1 cup of water, cover, and allow it to simmer for about 10 minutes. Add cauliflower to the sauce, adding more water if needed. Cover and allow to simmer for 25 to 30 minutes, or until cauliflower is tender. Remove from the heat; discard cinnamon, bay leaves, and rosemary; and serve hot or cold.

◆ *Serves 5 to 6*

Eggplant Ragout

MELIZANES YIAHNI

1½ to 2 pounds small Italian
   eggplants
Salt
¼ cup olive oil
1 large onion, chopped
3 cloves garlic, finely chopped
1 tablespoon chopped fresh basil

1 tablespoon chopped fresh mint
1 tablespoon chopped fresh
   parsley
4 to 5 ripe tomatoes, peeled and
   chopped, with juice
Salt and pepper
1 cup water

Remove stems from eggplant and cut into 1½-inch-round slices; then cut each slice into quarters. Place in a colander, sprinkle with salt, and allow to stand for 50 minutes. Rinse with cold water 2 or 3 times and pat dry. In a large saucepan, heat oil and sauté onion and garlic until soft. Add eggplant slices and sauté for 7 to 8 minutes, then add basil, mint, and parsley and stir 2 or 3 times. Add tomatoes, salt and pepper, and 1 cup water and reduce heat to medium. Cover and simmer for 50 minutes to 1 hour, or until the eggplant is tender and the sauce thickens; add a little water if necessary. This is great with feta cheese and crusty bread or on any type of pasta, with a sprinkle of grated Parmesan cheese.

◆ *Serves 4 to 5*

Fried Eggplant with Tomato Sauce

Melizanes Tiganites me Saltsa

S erve this delicious dish during summer with bread and a salad.

2 large eggplants
Salt

Olive oil, for frying

Batter:

1 cup flour
1½ cups milk

1 egg
Pinch of salt

Tomato sauce:

3 tablespoons olive oil
½ cup finely chopped onion
3 cloves garlic, thinly sliced
1½ cups peeled and crushed fresh
    tomatoes
1 teaspoon tomato paste

1 tablespoon chopped fresh basil
Salt and pepper
½ cup water
½ cup grated kefalotyri or
    Parmesan cheese

Slice eggplant into ½-inch-round slices, place the slices in a large colander, and sprinkle with salt. Allow to drain for 50 minutes, then rinse with cold water and pat dry. In a large skillet, heat about ¾ inch of olive oil. Meanwhile, put the flour and a pinch of salt in a shallow dish plate. In a medium bowl, beat milk and egg, then dip eggplant slices into the egg mixture. Dip each egg-covered eggplant slice into the flour, shaking off the excess. Fry eggplant slices in hot oil for 3 to 5 minutes on each side until golden brown. Remove from the skillet with a slotted spoon and drain on paper towels. Into a small saucepan add 3 tablespoons of olive oil and sauté onion and garlic for 5 minutes. Add tomatoes, tomato paste, basil, salt and pepper, and ½ cup water. Reduce heat to medium and simmer for 25 minutes, or until sauce is thickened. Place eggplant slices on a large platter and spoon the tomato sauce over them. Sprinkle with the cheese and serve hot.

◆ *Serves 4*

Green Beans with Zucchini

Fasolakia me Kolokithakia

1 to 1½ pounds string beans or
    flat green beans
¼ cup olive oil
1 large onion, finely chopped
3 cloves garlic, chopped
3 to 4 fresh tomatoes, skinned and
    chopped, or 1 cup canned
    crushed tomatoes

1½ cups water
3 medium zucchini, cut into 2-inch
    pieces and stems removed
2 tablespoons chopped fresh
    parsley
1 tablespoon chopped fresh mint
Salt and freshly ground pepper

Trim the green beans (string them if necessary), cut in half, wash, and drain. In a large saucepan, heat oil and sauté the onion and garlic for 5 minutes. Add green beans and sauté for 7 to 8 minutes. Add tomatoes and 1½ cups of water and simmer for 30 to 40 minutes. Add zucchini, parsley, mint, salt and pepper, and more water if necessary and cook for 25 minutes, or until beans and zucchini are tender. Remove from the heat and allow to stand for 10 minutes. Serve with feta cheese, kalamata olives, and crusty bread.

◆ *Serves 4*

Lemon Fava Beans with Artichokes

KOUKIA ME AGINARES

1½ to 2 pounds fresh fava beans,
   shelled
¼ cup olive oil
1 cup chopped scallions
½ cup chopped fresh dill
2 tablespoons chopped fresh parsley

1½ cups water
Salt and pepper
2 (14-ounce) cans artichoke hearts,
   drained
Juice of 1 to 2 lemons
Chopped parsley or dill, for garnish

Chill the beans, place in a colander, rinse with water, and drain. In a large saucepan, heat olive oil, add scallions, and sauté, stirring continuously, for 3 to 4 minutes. Add fava beans and stir for 5 minutes, then add dill, parsley, 1½ cups water, and salt and pepper. Cover and cook over medium heat for about 40 minutes. Add artichoke hearts and lemon juice and cook for 10 more minutes, adding more water if necessary. Remove from heat and serve hot or cold sprinkled with chopped dill or parsley. This dish is a great spring meal and is delicious with marinated feta cheese and olives.

♦ *Serves 4*

Lemon Roast Potatoes

Patates Psites

This is a delicious side dish.

5 to 6 large baking potatoes	1 teaspoon chopped fresh rosemary
Juice of 2 lemons	1 bay leaf
¼ cup olive oil	Salt and pepper
3 cloves garlic, minced	1 cup chicken stock
1 teaspoon dried oregano	1 teaspoon paprika

Preheat the oven to 350 degrees. Peel, wash, and quarter the potatoes and put them in a medium baking pan. In a bowl, mix lemon juice, oil, garlic, oregano, rosemary, bay leaf, and salt and pepper. Beat with a fork and pour over the potatoes, then add the chicken stock. Sprinkle with paprika and roast for about 1½ hours until potatoes turn a golden brown. If they start to dry out, add a little water. Serve hot as a side dish.

◆ *Serves 4 to 5*

Meatless Stuffed Peppers and Tomatoes with Rice

GEMISTA ME RIZI

This is my favorite meatless dish, especially in the summer with garden-fresh tomatoes and peppers.

6 to 8 firm ripe medium tomatoes

6 to 8 small green bell peppers

¼ cup olive oil

1 cup finely chopped onion

3 cloves garlic, minced

2 tablespoons chopped fresh basil

2 tablespoons chopped fresh mint

¼ cup chopped fresh parsley

1 cup uncooked long-grain white rice

1 cup fresh crushed tomatoes

1¼ cups water

Salt and pepper

½ cup grated Parmesan cheese

3 large baking potatoes, peeled and quartered

½ teaspoon dried oregano

Salt and pepper

½ cup canned crushed tomatoes

2 tablespoons olive oil

Preheat the oven to 350 degrees. Wash tomatoes and peppers and pat them dry, then, with a sharp knife, slice off the tops and reserve. Seed the peppers and, using a teaspoon, gently scoop the pulp out of the tomatoes. Chop the pulp and place in a bowl. In a medium saucepan, heat olive oil and sauté onion, garlic, basil, mint, and parsley for 5 minutes. Add rice and cook, stirring frequently, until lightly browned. Stir in tomato pulp, fresh crushed tomatoes, 1 cup of the water, and salt and pepper to taste, cover, and allow to simmer over low heat for 8 to 10 minutes, until the rice is softened but not cooked and most of the liquid is absorbed. Remove from the stove and allow to cool for 10 minutes, then stir in cheese. Using a tablespoon, fill tomatoes and peppers, then place them in a baking pan. Cover each tomato and pepper with its top that you cut off. Arrange potatoes around the tomatoes and peppers and sprinkle them with oregano and salt and pepper. Add canned crushed tomatoes and ¼ cup of water and drizzle oil on top. Bake for 1½ hours, or until vegetables are tender and brown on top, basting occasionally with pan juices. Serve warm. Be sure to serve this delicious dish with feta cheese and a salad.

◆ *Serves 6*

Potatoes Yiahni

PATATES KOKINISTES

This is a good side dish.

6 large potatoes

¼ cup olive oil

1 cup finely chopped onion

4 cloves garlic, chopped

1 large green bell pepper, chopped

1 tablespoon chopped fresh parsley

1 teaspoon dried oregano

½ teaspoon dried mint

3 to 4 fresh peeled tomatoes, crushed, or 1 cup canned crushed tomatoes

2 cups water

2 bay leaves

Salt and pepper

Wash, peel, and quarter potatoes. In a large pot, heat oil and sauté onion and garlic for 5 minutes, or until soft. Add potatoes and green pepper and sauté 10 minutes. Stir in parsley, oregano, mint, tomatoes, water, bay leaves, and salt and pepper, then cover and simmer for 1 hour, or until potatoes are tender, adding more water if necessary. This delicious dish should be served with bread for dunking.

♦ *Serves 5 to 6*

Rice with Spinach and Lemon

Spanakorizo me Lemoni

2 (10-ounce) packages fresh
    spinach
¼ cup olive oil
1 large onion, finely chopped
½ cup chopped scallions
½ cup chopped fresh fennel with
    leaves

½ cup chopped fresh dill
1 tablespoon chopped fresh parsley
Salt and pepper
1½ cups water
½ cup uncooked long-grain
    white rice
Juice of 2 lemons

Clean and rinse spinach leaves 2 or 3 times in plenty of cold water. Drain and cut each leaf into 3 or 4 pieces. Heat oil in a medium saucepan, add onion and scallions, and sauté until tender. Add spinach, fennel, dill, and parsley and stir a few times until the spinach is wilted, then add salt and pepper and water. Cover and allow to simmer for 15 minutes. Add the rice and stir well so rice does not stick to the pan. Cover again and allow to simmer for 20 to 25 minutes, or until rice is tender, adding more water if necessary. Stir in lemon juice, remove from heat, and allow to stand for 10 minutes. Serve with bread and feta cheese.

◆ *Serves 4 to 5*

String Beans with Potatoes

Fasolakia me Patates Yiahni

Although this delicious dish can be served alone, it also makes a lovely side dish.

1 pound fresh string beans

3 medium potatoes

¼ cup olive oil

1 large onion, chopped

3 cloves garlic, chopped

2 tablespoons chopped fresh parsley

1 tablespoon chopped fresh mint

2 carrots, sliced

2 celery stalks, finely chopped

2 large tomatoes, peeled and chopped

1 cup canned crushed tomatoes

2 cups water

Salt and freshly ground pepper

Wash and trim beans, then cut them in half; wash and peel potatoes and quarter them. In a large saucepan, heat oil and sauté onion, garlic, parsley, and mint for 3 minutes. Add beans, carrots, celery, and potatoes and sauté for 10 minutes. Add chopped tomatoes, crushed tomatoes, 2 cups of water, and salt and freshly ground pepper to taste. Stir 2 or 3 times, cover, and reduce heat to medium. Cook for 1 hour, or until vegetables are tender and most of the water has evaporated. Serve hot or cold with feta cheese and bread.

◆ *Serves 6*

Stuffed Zucchini with Rice

Kolokithakia Yemista me Rizi

10 medium zucchini

¼ cup olive oil

1 large onion, finely chopped

4 cloves garlic, finely chopped

1 cup uncooked long-grain
   white rice

¼ cup finely chopped fresh parsley

2 tablespoons chopped fresh mint

3 large ripe tomatoes, peeled and
   chopped, with juice

¼ cup pine nuts, toasted

Salt and pepper

2 cups water, divided

3 tablespoons grated Parmesan
   cheese

¾ cup peeled and chopped fresh
   tomatoes, with juice

2 tablespoons olive oil

Mint sprigs, for garnish

Preheat the oven to 350 degrees. Wash zucchini well and cut off stems. With a potato peeler, carefully scoop out the insides of the zucchini and chop; set aside. In a large heavy skillet, heat oil and sauté onion, garlic, and chopped zucchini for 2 to 3 minutes until soft. Add rice, parsley, and mint, and stir until rice is lightly browned. Stir in tomatoes, pine nuts, salt and pepper, and 1½ cups of the water, reduce heat to low, and simmer until rice is softened but not cooked through. Remove from heat and place rice mixture in a large bowl; add Parmesan cheese and cool slightly. Using a teaspoon, fill hollow zucchini with rice mixture and place them in a baking pan. Pour ¾ cup of tomatoes over zucchini; drizzle with oil, add a ½ cup of water, and season with salt and pepper to taste. Cover the pan and bake for 50 minutes, then remove cover and bake uncovered for 30 more minutes, or until zucchini is golden on top. Remove from oven and allow to stand for 10 minutes. Garnish with mint sprigs and serve with a Greek salad and bread.

◆ *Serves 5*

Vegetarian Stuffed Cabbage with Egg and Lemon Sauce

DOLMATHES ME RIZI AVGOLEMONO

1 large cabbage (2½ to 3 pounds)

¼ cup olive oil

1 large onion, finely chopped

½ cup finely chopped celery

2 cloves garlic, minced

½ cup finely chopped carrots

2 cups uncooked long-grain
   white rice

2 cups vegetable stock or water,
   plus extra for final cooking

¼ cup chopped fresh flat
   parsley

2 tablespoons chopped fresh dill

2 egg whites, lightly beaten

½ cup pine nuts

2 tablespoons dark seedless raisins
   (optional)

Salt and pepper

2 tablespoons olive oil

Remove any yellow leaves from cabbage and blanch the head in a large pot of boiling water for 25 minutes, or until all the leaves are softened. Set aside to drain and cool. When cool enough to handle, remove the leaves one by one and set aside. In a medium saucepan, heat oil and sauté onion, celery, garlic, and carrots for 7 minutes. Add rice and cook, stirring with a wooden spoon, for 3 minutes, or until lightly browned. Add stock and cook until rice is softened but not cooked through. Remove to a large bowl and allow to cool slightly. When it has cooled, add parsley, dill, egg whites, pine nuts, raisins, and salt and pepper and mix well. Place 1½ to 2 table-spoons of stuffing near the base of each cabbage leaf, then fold in the sides and roll up. Place 3 large cabbage leaves on the bottom of a large saucepan, add the stuffed rolls open side down, and sprinkle them with salt and pepper to taste. Pour olive oil over all, then add enough vegetable stock or water to cover. Place a plate on top of the rolls; cover the pot, and simmer over medium heat for 1½ hours, or until the cabbage and rice are tender, adding water if necessary. Remove pot from the heat.

Egg and lemon sauce:

2 cups vegetable stock

2 eggs

Juice of 2 lemons

1 teaspoon cornstarch

Salt and pepper

Bring vegetable stock to a boil in a small saucepan. In a blender, beat 2 eggs, lemon juice, and cornstarch; then, with the machine running slowly, add hot stock. Return egg mixture to the saucepan and stir over low heat until sauce has thickened. Then pour sauce over cabbage rolls and serve hot.

◆ *Serves 5 to 6*

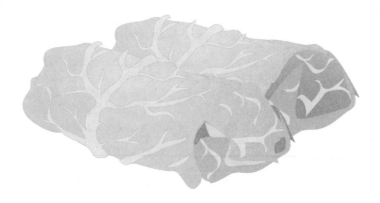

Vegetarian Stuffed Grape Leaves with Rice

DOLMATHAKIA ME RIZI

This is a delicious appetizer or side dish served warm or cold.

¼ cup plus 1 tablespoon olive oil

1 cup grated onion

½ cup finely chopped scallions

1½ cups uncooked long-grain
   white rice

2 tablespoons finely chopped fresh
   parsley

3 tablespoons finely chopped
   fresh mint

½ cup pine nuts, toasted

2 cups water

Salt and pepper

1 jar (16 ounces) grape leaves

Juice of 1½ lemons

Lemon slices, for garnish

In a medium-size saucepan, heat ¼ cup of oil, then add onion and scallions and sauté for 2 to 3 minutes until soft. Add rice and stir for 1 minute. Add parsley, mint, pine nuts, 2 cups of water, and salt and pepper, stirring 2 or 3 times. Reduce heat to medium-low and simmer for 10 minutes, or until the liquid is absorbed. Remove from heat and allow rice mixture to cool. Rinse grape leaves with cold water, drain, and trim tough stems. Cover bottom of a medium saucepan with 5 large grape leaves. Take 2 teaspoons of rice mixture and place at the base of each leaf, then fold in the sides and roll up. Place rolls close together in layers in the saucepan. Sprinkle with salt and pepper, 1 tablespoon olive oil, and lemon juice and add enough water to cover the rolls. Place a plate over rolls, cover, and cook over medium heat for 1 hour, or until the grape leaves are tender and all the water has evaporated. Remove from heat and allow to cool. Arrange on a large platter and garnish with lemon slices. Serve with tzatziki sauce (Cucumber Yogurt Dip, page 8).

◆ *Serves 6*

Zucchini Ragout

Kolokithakia Yiahni

This dish can be served as a main course with feta cheese and bread. It's also delicious on top of pasta or rice.

1½ to 2 pounds small zucchini

¼ cup olive oil

1 large onion, chopped

3 cloves garlic, chopped

2 tablespoons chopped fresh parsley

2 tablespoons chopped fresh mint

3 large tomatoes, peeled and chopped, with juice

2 teaspoons tomato paste

1 cup water

Salt and pepper

Wash zucchini well, remove stems, and pat dry, then cut into 1-inch pieces. In a large saucepan, heat oil and sauté onion and garlic for 5 minutes, or until soft. Add zucchini to the onions and stir for 5 minutes, then add parsley, mint, tomatoes, tomato paste, water, and salt and pepper. Cover and simmer over medium-low heat for 45 minutes, or until zucchini is tender and sauce has thickened. Remove from heat and serve hot or cold.

◆ *Serves 4 to 5*

OLIVE OIL

I was born and raised in Greece, but I am an American now, a Greek American. In the Old Country, we used lots of butter and oil and spent hours preparing meals. But Americans are busy and health conscious, and I want my recipes to help you prepare easy but nutritious meals that fit your lifestyle. My recipes are Greek with an American twist, just like me.

In addition to the freshest vegetables, fruits, herbs, and spices, I emphasize the use of olive oil. The aroma of olive oil fills my house with its light fragrance and enhances my mouthwatering food. Olive oil is healthy and delicious and is rapidly finding its way into the American diet.

Olive oil is as old as Greece and has been used as a culinary oil for thousands of years. It is said that the goddess Athena planted the first olive tree on the site of the Acropolis, and that the olive tree growing there today comes from that tree's original roots. The olive and the olive branch also have deep historical roots in Greece, representing reconciliation, peace, and prosperity. "Extending the olive branch," the symbol of conciliation, represents a powerful human emotion. The traditional crown of olive leaves, placed on the heads of victorious athletes, represents bravery.

It takes fifty years to establish an olive tree, but they live for three hundred to four hundred years, some as long as seven hundred years. Olive groves cover the sunny hillsides of my native home in Peloponnese. I like to say that I grew up with olive trees. My father, who is ninety-two, still has acres of olive groves. I know olives.

Types of Olive Oil

There are many types of olive oil, each with its own aroma and taste. Differences in olive oil result from the variety of olives used, the year (much like fine wine, there are "good" years and "bad" years) and location in which they are grown, how ripe the olives are when converted to oil (the greener the better), and the acidity of the oil. Olive oil should never be bitter, have a strong odor, or leave an aftertaste. Olive oil is produced in Greece, Spain, Italy, and California; if you specifically want Greek olive oil, see that the container is marked as such.

Premium Select Extra-Virgin Olive Oil. This is the highest grade and has very low acidity. The olives are hand harvested and pressed within twenty-four hours.

Extra-Virgin Olive Oil. Extra-virgin is a low-acid oil produced by the first pressing of the olive.

Virgin Olive Oil. Made from slightly riper olives, it has a higher acidity level than extra-virgin olive oil.

Pure Olive Oil. A general-purpose olive oil, it is lighter and blander than virgin olive oil.

Buying and Storing Olive Oil

Before you settle on an olive oil, buy a few small bottles for tasting. Once you've chosen your favorite, you can purchase olive oil in large containers, but it should be decanted and stored in smaller containers in a cool, dark place.

Light and heat are the enemies of olive oil, and stored improperly, it can easily go bad. Store olive oil in a dark glass or tin container away from heat. It may be stored in the refrigerator, but it will turn almost solid and you will have to warm it to room temperature before you use it. Storing olive oil in the refrigerator, however, will extend the life of the oil.

The Many Uses of Olive Oil

Raw olive oil enhances many recipes, bringing out the natural flavors of other ingredients and reducing acidity. Americans, increasingly aware of its health benefits, are using olive oil for salad dressings, sauces, marinades, bread dipping, drizzling on food, and baking. Used for frying, sautéing, and searing, olive oil remains stable and, unlike the more commonly used seed oils, does not smoke at high temperatures.

Georgia's olive oil label.

Chicken Dishes

- Aromatic Grilled Chicken with Wine   104
- Chicken Casserole with Egg Noodles   105
- Chicken Croquettes   106
- Chicken Stew with Peppers   107
- Chicken Stew with Potatoes   108
- Chicken Stew with Rice   109
- Chicken-Stuffed Grape Leaves   110
- Delicious Moussaka with Chicken   111
- Georgia's Garlic Chicken Wings   113
- Grecian Chicken Kabobs with Vegetables   114
- Grilled Chicken Beefteki   116
- Lemon Chicken with Potatoes   117
- Oven-Fried Chicken Breast   118
- Roasted Chicken with Potatoes and Onions   120
- Stuffed Chicken with Mushrooms and Rice   121
- Stuffed Turkey with Chestnuts   123

Aromatic Grilled Chicken with Wine

Aromatiki Kota sta Karvouna

The mouthwatering aroma of this chicken dish gives it its unforgettable taste.

Marinade:

¾ cup white wine

¼ cup olive oil

1½ tablespoons finely chopped
   fresh basil

½ teaspoon dried mint

1 tablespoon dried oregano

1 bay leaf, crushed

3 cloves garlic, finely chopped

1 teaspoon paprika

Salt and freshly ground pepper

In a large bowl, combine wine, oil, basil, mint, oregano, bay leaf, garlic, paprika, and salt and pepper to taste. Mix well.

1 broiler/fryer chicken (2½ to 3 pounds)

Cut chicken halfway down the backbone, then press down on the breast to flatten the halves slightly. Add chicken halves to marinade and turn to coat thoroughly. Cover and refrigerate for 3 to 6 hours. Preheat grill on high; when it's hot, remove chicken from marinade, reserving the liquid. Place skin side down on grill rack about 5 to 6 inches above the coals and grill for 25 minutes. Turn and brush with marinade; cover the grill and turn it to down to medium heat. Grill chicken for 25 to 35 minutes more, until the chicken is tender and no pink remains. Serve with tossed salad, rice pilaf, and tzatziki sauce.

◆ *Serves 4*

Chicken Casserole with Egg Noodles

KOTA STO FOURNO ME HILOPITES

Chicken casserole with egg noodles is a traditional Sunday Greek meal. When I was a child, I remember, my sister Sofia would always look forward to Sundays to see if my mother had prepared her favorite dish. Today, Sofia prepares this dish all the time for her family because she can't get enough of it.

1 whole chicken (3½ to 4 pounds)

¼ cup olive oil

1 large onion, grated

3 cloves garlic, finely chopped

½ cup white wine

1½ cups fresh crushed tomatoes or
    canned whole plum tomatoes,
    crushed

1 cinnamon stick

1 bay leaf

Salt and pepper

4 cups water, divided

12 ounces uncooked egg noodles

½ cup grated kefalotyri or
    Parmesan cheese

Preheat the oven to 350 degrees. Remove the skin and fat from chicken, wash, cut into pieces, and pat dry. In a large saucepan, heat oil and brown chicken on all sides. Add onion and garlic and sauté for 5 minutes. Add wine and cook, stirring, for 2 minutes. Remove from heat and place chicken in a baking pan. Add tomatoes on top of the chicken, along with cinnamon, bay leaf, salt and pepper, and 2 cups of the water. Cover with foil and bake for 1½ hours. After removing pan from the oven, place noodles around the chicken pieces, stir well, and add 2 more cups of water and salt and pepper to taste. Cover and bake for about 30 minutes more, stirring occasionally, checking for dryness, and adding more water if necessary, until the chicken and noodles are tender. Make sure all the water has evaporated. Before serving, sprinkle with grated cheese. Serve hot with any green vegetable or a salad.

♦ *Serves 6*

Chicken Croquettes

BIFTEKIA ME KOTA

These delicious chicken croquettes make a great pocket sandwich—just add lettuce, tomatoes, onions, and tzatziki sauce. If you want a different kind of sandwich, try this—you'll love it!

1½ pounds chicken breast, cut into very small pieces

1 onion, grated

2 tablespoons chopped fresh parsley

1 tablespoon finely chopped fresh mint

3 cloves garlic, minced

1 egg white

½ cup soft bread crumbs

1 teaspoon dried oregano

Salt and pepper

¾ cup flour

½ cup olive oil, for frying

Parsley sprigs, for garnish

In a medium bowl, combine chicken, onion, parsley, mint, garlic, egg, bread crumbs, oregano, and salt and pepper. Knead the mixture, then cover and refrigerator for 1 hour. Use small quantities of the mixture to form flat croquettes and flour them lightly. Heat oil over medium heat in a large frying pan and fry croquettes on both sides until golden brown. Drain on paper towels, then arrange on a platter and garnish with parsley sprigs.

♦ *Serves 4*

Chicken Stew with Peppers

KOTA ME PIPERGIES

Serve this delicious dish with rice or your favorite pasta.

1 whole chicken (3½ to 4 pounds)
¼ cup olive oil
1 cup chopped onion
3 cloves garlic, chopped
2 medium green bell peppers,
  sliced into long strips
1 large red bell pepper, sliced into
  long strips
½ cup white dry wine

1½ cups peeled and crushed fresh
  tomatoes or canned crushed
  plum tomatoes
1 tablespoon chopped fresh flat
  parsley
1½ teaspoons chopped fresh thyme
2 bay leaves
Salt and pepper
1 cup water

Remove skin and trim excess fat from chicken, then wash, cut into pieces, and drain. In a large saucepan, heat oil and brown chicken on all sides. Add onion, garlic, and bell peppers and sauté for 5 minutes. Add wine and cook for 1 to 2 more minutes, then add tomatoes, parsley, thyme, bay leaves, salt and pepper, and water. Cover and simmer over low heat for 1 hour, or until chicken is tender and water has evaporated. Add more water if necessary during cooking. Serve hot.

◆ *Serves 5 to 6*

Chicken Stew with Potatoes

KOTA STIFATHO

Chicken stew with potatoes is great with crusty bread, feta cheese on the side, and a glass of wine.

1 whole chicken (3½ to 4 pounds)	½ cup canned crushed tomatoes
¼ cup olive oil	1 cinnamon stick
10 small whole new potatoes	1 bay leaf
10 small whole white onions	2 whole cloves
4 cloves garlic, peeled	Salt and freshly ground pepper
½ cup white wine	1½ cups chicken broth
8 ounces tomato sauce	2 tablespoons wine vinegar

After removing its skin, cut chicken into pieces, wash, and drain. Heat olive oil in a large pot and sauté chicken until lightly browned. Remove from pot and reserve. Peel the potatoes and onions, then wash and pat dry. Add to the pot, along with the garlic, and sauté, stirring, for 6 to 7 minutes. Add chicken to the pot, along with the wine, and stir 2 or 3 times. Stir in tomato sauce, tomatoes, cinnamon, bay leaf, cloves, salt and pepper, and 1½ cups of chicken broth. Cover, reduce heat to medium-low, and allow it to simmer for 1½ hours, or until the chicken is cooked. Check occasionally to make sure there is still liquid in the pot, adding a little more water if necessary. Add vinegar about 10 minutes before serving. Serve this delicious dish hot.

♦ *Serves 6*

Chicken Stew with Rice

Kota Yiahni me Rizi

One of my favorite dishes, this stew is so easy to make.

1 whole chicken (3½ to 4 pounds)
¼ cup olive oil
1 large onion, finely chopped
3 cloves garlic, finely chopped
1½ cup peeled and crushed fresh
    tomatoes
1 tablespoon tomato paste
¼ cup white wine

1 cinnamon stick
Salt and pepper
4 cups water
2 cups uncooked long-grain
    white rice
½ cup grated kefalotyri or
    Parmesan cheese

Remove skin and trim excess fat from the chicken, then wash, cut into pieces, and drain. In a large pot, heat oil and brown chicken on all sides. Add onion and garlic and sauté until tender. Stir in tomatoes, tomato paste, wine, cinnamon, salt and pepper, and 4 cups of water. Cover and simmer for 1 hour, then add rice and stir for 5 minutes. Add a little more salt to taste. Simmer over medium-low heat for 30 to 35 minutes, stirring occasionally, until the chicken and rice are tender. Add more water if necessary. Remove from the heat and let stand for 5 minutes. Sprinkle with cheese and serve with Greek salad.

◆ *Serves 5 to 6*

Chicken-Stuffed Grape Leaves

Kota Dolmathakia

Chicken-stuffed grape leaves are delicious and healthy; these are great as a meal or as an appetizer.

2 pounds ground chicken breast
1 large onion, grated
2 tablespoons chopped fresh mint
1 tablespoon chopped fresh
   parsley
2 cloves garlic, minced
1 large tomato, skinned, seeded,
   and chopped

½ cup uncooked long-grain
   white rice
1 egg, beaten
Salt and freshly ground pepper
1 jar (16 ounces) grape leaves
3 tablespoons olive oil
Juice of 1 lemon
Lemon slices, for garnish

In a large bowl, combine ground chicken, onion, mint, parsley, garlic, tomatoes, rice, egg, and salt and pepper; mix thoroughly and set aside for 15 minutes. Rinse and drain the grape leaves and trim stems. Use 5 large grape leaves to cover the bottom of a large saucepan. Take 1 tablespoon of stuffing, place it at base of each leaf, fold in the sides, and roll up. Place rolls close together in layers in the saucepan. Add more salt and pepper to taste, sprinkle with olive oil and lemon juice, add enough water (1½ to 2 cups) to cover, and put a plate over rolls. Cover pan and simmer for 1 hour or until chicken is tender and water has evaporated. Remove from heat and let stand for 15 to 20 minutes. Garnish with lemon slices and serve warm or cold.

◆ *Serves 5 to 6*

Delicious Moussaka with Chicken

MOUSSAKA ME KOTA

Moussaka is one of the national dishes of Greece. Chicken moussaka is very similar to the original moussaka; try this moussaka with chicken, and you'll never forget Georgia the Greek.

4 large eggplants

¼ cup olive oil, plus extra for frying
   the eggplants

1 cup onion, finely chopped

3 cloves garlic, finely chopped

¼ cup finely chopped fresh flat
   parsley

2 tablespoons finely chopped
   fresh mint

1½ to 2 pounds extra-lean ground
   chicken

½ cup dry wine

½ teaspoon ground cinnamon

2 cloves garlic, peeled

1 cup canned crushed tomatoes,
   with juice

Salt and pepper

2 tablespoons dried bread crumbs

¾ cup grated kefalotyri or
   Parmesan cheese, divided

Georgia-Style Béchamel Sauce
   (see page 68)

Preheat the oven to 350 degrees. Peel eggplants, then slice them lengthwise into ½-inch slices. Sprinkle with salt and let stand for 1 hour. Rinse with cold water and pat dry. Heat 1 inch of oil in large skillet and fry eggplant slices on both sides until light brown. Drain well on paper towels and set aside. Heat ¼ cup oil in a medium pot; add onion, garlic, parsley, and mint, and sauté for 5 minutes, or until soft. Add the ground chicken and sauté until barely brown. Add wine, stirring continuously to break up any lumps. Stir in cinnamon, cloves, tomatoes with their juice, and salt and pepper. Cover and simmer over low heat for 25 minutes, or until the liquid is absorbed. Remove from the stove and let cool for 10 minutes. Add bread crumbs and ¼ cup of cheese and mix well. Arrange half of the eggplant slices in the bottom of a 10 × 15 × 3-inch baking pan, sprinkle with ¼ cup cheese, and cover eggplant slices with an even layer of chicken mixture. Layer remaining eggplant slices on top of chicken mixture and sprinkle with cheese. Make a béchamel sauce. Spread béchamel sauce over eggplant slices and sprinkle with remaining ¼ cup of cheese. Bake for 50 minutes to 1 hour, or until the top is a golden brown. Remove from oven and cool for 20 minutes before cutting. This is delicious dish with salad and bread.

◆ *Serves 6 to 8*

Note: To reduce the number of calories, broil or grill the eggplants and proceed with the recipe directions.

Georgia's Garlic Chicken Wings

Fterougies me Skordo

Try these delicious chicken wings as an appetizer.

2½ to 3 pounds chicken wings
¾ cup olive oil, plus oil for baking
6 garlic cloves, peeled
Juice of 1 lemon
1 tablespoon fresh oregano
1 teaspoon fresh rosemary

4 drops Tabasco sauce
Salt and pepper
1½ cups plain bread crumbs
½ cup grated Parmesan cheese
1 teaspoon paprika
Lemon slices, for garnish

Preheat the oven to 375 degrees. Remove tips of chicken wings, then wash and pat them dry. Add oil, garlic, lemon juice, oregano, rosemary, Tabasco sauce, and salt and pepper to the bowl of a food processor or a blender and process until smooth. Pour sauce into a medium bowl and set aside. Combine bread crumbs, cheese, and paprika in a shallow dish. Dip wings one at time in garlic mixture, then roll in bread crumb mixture until thoroughly coated. Brush a nonstick baking pan with oil, then add wings in a single layer. Bake for 1 hour, or until wings are brown and crisp. Remove from the oven and let stand for 10 minutes before serving. Garnish with lemon slices.

◆ *Serves 6*

Grecian Chicken Kabobs with Vegetables

Kota Souvlaki

Popular in Greece, souvlaki is usually made with lamb or pork, but try it with chicken; it's good for you and delicious.

1½ pounds boneless, skinless chicken breast, cut into large chunks

1 red bell pepper, cut into 1-inch pieces

2 small zucchini, cut into 1-inch pieces

10 cherry tomatoes

1 onion, cut into wedges

Olive oil, to brush grill

1 package rice pilaf

½ cup crumbled feta cheese

Chopped parsley, for garnish

Marinade:

Juice of 2 lemons

¼ cup olive oil

1 teaspoon finely chopped fresh rosemary

1 tablespoon chopped fresh oregano

4 cloves garlic, finely chopped

Salt and freshly ground pepper

In a large bowl, combine lemon juice, olive oil, rosemary, oregano, garlic, and salt and pepper to taste. Add chicken and stir to coat with marinade, then cover and refrigerate for 3 hours. Remove chicken from the marinade, reserving the liquid. Thread chicken, pepper, zucchini, tomatoes, and onion alternately on each of 5 or 6 skewers, leaving a little space between pieces. Preheat grill and brush with oil. Grill kabobs over medium heat 12 minutes on each side, turning and brushing frequently with the marinade until chicken is no longer pink. Prepare rice according to package directions. Mound rice in the middle of a large platter, arrange chicken kabobs around rice, and sprinkle with feta cheese and chopped parsley. Serve hot with salad.

◆ *Serves 5 to 6*

Grilled Chicken Beefteki

Kota Bifteki sta Karvouna

Here is another easy and light dish for dinner.

1 to 1½ pounds ground chicken
    breast
1 large onion, grated
1 large tomato, peeled, seeded,
    and chopped
3 cloves garlic, minced
2 tablespoons finely chopped
    fresh basil

1 tablespoon finely chopped
    fresh parsley
½ teaspoon dried oregano
1 tablespoon lemon juice
1 egg white, lightly beaten
½ cup plain bread crumbs
Salt and pepper
Olive oil, to brush grill

In a large bowl, combine chicken, onion, tomato, garlic, basil, parsley, oregano, lemon juice, egg white, bread crumbs, and salt and pepper. Mix very well with your hands, then cover and refrigerator for 1 hour. While the grill preheats, make 4 or 5 large patties. Oil the grill and cook the patties 10 minutes on each side, or until cooked through. Arrange the patties on a platter and serve with tzatziki sauce, rice pilaf, and a salad.

◆ *Serves 4 to 5*

Lemon Chicken with Potatoes

LEMONATI KOTA ME PATATES

1 whole chicken (3½ to 4 pounds)

¼ cup olive oil

8 to 10 small gourmet white
   potatoes, peeled

4 cloves garlic, crushed

Juice of 2 to 3 fresh lemons

1 tablespoon chopped fresh oregano

½ teaspoon dried thyme

Salt and pepper

1½ cups water

Chopped parsley, for garnish

Lemon slices, for garnish

Remove skin and any excess fat from chicken, then wash it, cut it into pieces, and pat dry. In a large saucepan, heat oil and lightly fry chicken. Remove chicken pieces from saucepan and reserve. Peel and wash potatoes and pat them dry, then put them in a skillet and fry them lightly. Remove from the skillet and reserve. Add 1 tablespoon of oil to skillet and lightly sauté garlic. Add chicken pieces to the skillet, then add lemon juice, oregano, thyme, salt and pepper, and water and bring to a boil. Reduce heat to medium and simmer for 50 minutes to 1 hour. Arrange potatoes around the chicken, adding a more little water if necessary, and cook until chicken and potatoes are done, the water has evaporated, and only sauce remains. Arrange chicken on a serving platter with the potatoes surrounding it. Sprinkle with chopped parsley and garnish with lemon slices.

◆ *Serves 5 to 6*

Oven-Fried Chicken Breast

STITHOS KOTAS PANE

T he marinade gives this chicken its mouthwatering essence.

4 to 5 chicken breast fillets,
    pounded lightly to an even
    thickness

Marinade:

Juice of 1½ lemons

¼ cup olive oil

3 cloves garlic, minced

1 teaspoon dried oregano

1 teaspoon finely chopped fresh
    rosemary

Salt and pepper

1 whole egg plus 2 egg whites

1 tablespoon water

1 cup flour

1 cup bread crumbs

Olive oil, to brush baking pan

1 teaspoon paprika

Lemon slices, for garnish

Parsley sprigs, for garnish

Place chicken breast fillets into a large bowl. In a medium bowl, mix lemon juice, oil, garlic, oregano, rosemary, and salt and pepper and pour marinade over chicken to coat thoroughly. Cover and refrigerate for 1 hour. Meanwhile, in a medium bowl, beat egg and egg whites with 1 tablespoon of water. Place flour and bread crumbs on separate plates, then coat each fillet with flour, dip into the egg mixture, and coat with bread crumbs. Brush a baking pan with oil, arrange fillets in pan, and sprinkle with paprika. Bake for 50 minutes to 1 hour, or until fillets are golden in color. Remove from the oven and cool for 5 minutes, then arrange them on a platter and garnish with lemon slices and parsley sprigs. Serve with artichokes, potato salad or rice pilaf, and a tossed salad.

◆ *Serves 4 to 5*

Note: You can use any chicken parts for this recipe, but if you're using dark meat, cook for 1½ hours, or until chicken is golden in color.

Roasted Chicken with Potatoes and Onions

KOTA STO FOURNO ME PATATES KAI KREMIDIA

This is a very easy dish to prepare, and you'll love it.

1 whole chicken (3½ to 4 pounds)

5 large baked potatoes, washed, peeled, and quartered

8 small white onions, peeled and washed

Marinade:

Juice of 2 fresh lemons

¼ cup olive oil

4 to 5 cloves garlic, minced

1/2 teaspoon dried oregano

1 teaspoon dried thyme

1½ teaspoon crushed dried rosemary

Salt and pepper

2 bay leaves

Preheat the oven to 350 degrees. Trim excess fat from chicken, wash, and drain. Place chicken in a large deep roasting pan. Arrange potatoes and onions around chicken in the baking pan. In a small jar, combine lemon juice, olive oil, garlic, oregano, thyme, rosemary, and salt and pepper and mix well. Pour marinade over the chicken, onion, and potatoes. Add bay leaves and season with more salt and pepper to taste. Add 1 cup of water to the pan and bake for 1½ to 2 hours, or until chicken and potatoes are golden brown on top, adding more water if needed and basting chicken with juices as it cooks. Remove from oven and let stand for 10 minutes. Arrange the chicken on a platter surrounded with potatoes and onions. Garnish with lemon slices and serve with salad or any greens.

◆ *Serves 5 to 6*

Stuffed Chicken with Mushrooms and Rice

KOTA YEMISTI ME MANITARIA KAI RIZI

Serve this delicious dish with any type of salad or greens.

1 large oven-roasted chicken
   (4½ to 5 pounds)
¼ cup plus 1 tablespoon olive oil
1 medium onion, finely chopped
1 celery stalk, finely chopped
¾ cup chopped fresh mushrooms
2 cloves garlic, crushed
1 cup uncooked long-grain
   white rice
2 medium ripe tomatoes, peeled
   and chopped, with juice
1½ cups chicken broth

1 tablespoon chopped fresh parsley
½ teaspoon dried mint
1 cinnamon stick
1 whole clove
½ cup pine nuts
Salt and pepper
Juice of 1 lemon
½ teaspoon dried oregano
½ teaspoon crushed dried
   rosemary
Salt and pepper
1 cup water

Preheat the oven to 350 degrees. Wash and trim excess fat from the chicken and drain. In a medium saucepan, heat ¼ cup of olive oil and sauté onion, celery, mushrooms, and garlic for 5 minutes. Add rice and cook, stirring, for 2 to 3 minutes until rice turns lightly golden. Add tomatoes, broth, parsley, mint, cinnamon, clove, pine nuts, and salt and pepper. Cover and simmer over low heat for about 10 minutes. Stir continuously until liquid is absorbed and rice is softened but not cooked through. Remove from stove and cool for 10 minutes. Fill chicken cavity with rice stuffing. Secure the opening with a toothpick and place chicken in a baking pan. In a medium bowl, mix lemon juice, 1 tablespoon of oil, oregano, rosemary, and salt and pepper and brush outside of the chicken with the marinade. Add 1 cup of water to the pan and bake for 1½ to 2 hours, or until the chicken is done, basting often. Add liquid to the pan if needed. When chicken has finished baking, remove from the oven and allow to stand for 10 minutes. Carefully pull out toothpicks and remove stuffing, then cut chicken into pieces. Place stuffing in the center of a serving platter and arrange chicken pieces around it. Spoon some pan liquid onto chicken.

♦ *Serves 6*

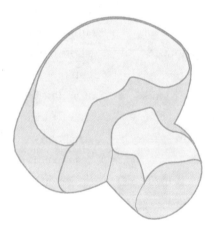

Stuffed Turkey with Chestnuts

Galopoula Yemisti me Kastana

S tuffed turkey with chestnuts was my mother's traditional Christmas
dish.

1 turkey (12 to 15 pounds)

Salt and pepper

Juice of 1 lemon

½ teaspoon dried oregano

Stuffing:

1 pound chestnuts

½ cup olive oil, divided

1 cup finely chopped onion

3 cloves garlic, crushed

1½ pounds ground beef

2 tablespoons chopped flat
   parsley

¼ cup brandy or wine

¾ cup uncooked long-grain
   white rice

½ cup pine nuts

¼ cup golden raisins

1 cinnamon stick

½ teaspoon ground cloves

Salt and pepper

1½ cups chicken broth

Preheat the oven to 350 degrees. Make a slit on flat side of each chestnut,
then place in a large pot with enough water to cover and boil until tender.
Remove from heat, and peel off the skin and fibers, being careful not to
break the nut. In a large pan, heat ¼ cup of the oil and sauté onion and garlic for 3 to 5 minutes. Add ground beef and parsley, stirring until lightly
browned. Add brandy and rice and continue stirring, then add pine nuts,
raisins, cinnamon, cloves, salt and pepper, and chicken broth. Simmer uncovered for 7 to 8 minutes, add chestnuts, and continue to simmer until liq-

uid is absorbed. Remove from heat and cool slightly. Remove cinnamon stick. Wash and trim excess fat from inside the turkey cavity and drain. Sprinkle with salt and pepper. Drizzle lemon juice and sprinkle oregano on the outside of the turkey. Fill the turkey cavity with stuffing and sew closed. Add remaining stuffing to neck cavity and close. Place turkey in a baking pan and drizzle with remaining ¼ cup of olive oil. Pour 1 cup of water into pan and bake for 3½ to 4 hours, or until turkey is tender and cooked through, basting with pan juices every 20 minutes. Remove pan from oven, allow turkey to cool slightly, and remove stuffing from cavity. Serve turkey on a large platter with stuffing around it.

◆ *Serves 8 to 10*

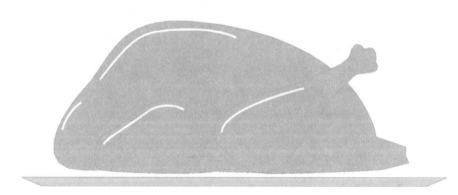

RED-DYED EGGS FOR EASTER

*E*aster is one of the most celebrated holidays in Greece; the festivities begin by dyeing eggs red. The dyed eggs are used in the Easter sweet bread and as a side dish for Easter dinner. The dinner begins with cracking the red eggs. Everyone chooses an egg, and all play a little game in which each person cracks his or her egg against another person's egg. The object of the game is to see who has the strongest egg. The person whose egg remains unbroken is thought to be the strongest person for the rest of the year.

25 to 30 white eggs   1 cup vinegar
1 envelope red egg dye

Wash the eggs with warm water and pat dry. Dissolve the dye in a 1 cup of boiled water. Fill a large pot with enough water to cover the eggs. Add vinegar and dissolved dye and bring to a boil. Skim the froth off the surface before adding the eggs to the pot. Boil the eggs for 20 to 25 minutes until they are hard-boiled. Remove them very carefully and place them on a platter, then polish them with a piece of cloth dipped in a little oil. The eggs will be a beautiful deep red.

Main Dishes

- Aromatic Braised Roast Beef   129
- Aromatic Lamb Kabobs   130
- Aromatic Lamb with Tomato Sauce and Pasta   131
- Baked Lamb with Potatoes   132
- Corfu Spicy Veal Stew with Pasta   133
- Delicious Pork Kabobs   134
- Delicious Pork with Leeks   135
- Georgia's Roasted Leg of Lamb   136
- Greek Lasagna   138
- Grilled Lamb Chops Stuffed with Feta Cheese   140
- Grilled Lamb Chops with Mint Marinade   142
- Grilled or Broiled Pork Chops   143
- Hamburgers Pane   144
- Hamburgers Stuffed with Feta Cheese   145
- Lamb Chops Pane   146
- Lamb Ragout with Potatoes   148
- Lamb with Spinach and Egg Lemon Sauce   149
- Lemon Garlic Roasted Pork Loin   151
- Meatballs with Tomato Sauce   152

- MEAT LOAF WITH FETA CHEESE   154
- MEAT LOAF ROLL STUFFED WITH EGGS   155
- MOUSSAKA   156
- OVEN-BAKED LAMB WITH ZUCCHINI   158
- PORK FRICASSEE   159
- ROASTED PORK WITH POTATOES   160
- ROASTED RACK OF LAMB WITH LEMON   162
- SAUSAGE WITH PEPPERS AND ONIONS   163
- SPICED PORK WITH CABBAGE IN TOMATO SAUCE   164
- STOVE-TOP ROASTED LAMB WITH LEMON   165
- STUFFED CABBAGE WITH EGG LEMON SAUCE   166
- STUFFED GRAPE LEAVES WITH EGG LEMON SAUCE   167
- STUFFED LEG OF LAMB WITH HAM AND CHEESE   169
- STUFFED ROMAINE LETTUCE WITH EGG AND LEMON SAUCE   171
- VEAL STEW WITH RICE PILAF   173

Aromatic Braised Roast Beef

Mosxari Kokinisto

This traditional recipe is great for a Sunday indulgence.

3½ to 4 pounds beef (eye round)

½ teaspoon ground cloves

½ teaspoon ground cinnamon

½ teaspoon salt

½ teaspoon pepper

5 to 6 cloves garlic, peeled

¼ cup olive oil

1 cup finely chopped onion

2 cloves garlic, finely chopped

½ cup red wine

1 can (8 ounces) tomato sauce

2 teaspoons tomato paste

1 teaspoon sugar

1 bay leaf

1 small cinnamon stick

1 tablespoon red wine vinegar

Salt and pepper

Wash and pat dry the meat. With a sharp knife, make small slits all over the meat. Combine cloves, cinnamon, and salt and pepper, then insert whole cloves of garlic and a pinch of the mixture into the slits and rub the meat with any of the remaining mixture. In a large pot, brown the meat in oil on all sides, then remove from the pan. Add onion and chopped garlic to the oil and sauté for 5 minutes or until soft. Return meat to the pan and add wine, tomato sauce, tomato paste, sugar, bay leaf, cinnamon stick, vinegar, and salt and pepper along with enough hot water to cover the meat. Cover and simmer for 1½ to 2 hours, or until meat is tender. Turn meat every 20 to 25 minutes, and add more water if necessary. Remove meat and place onto a platter and keep hot. Cook sauce until smooth and glossy. Slice meat, spoon the sauce over it, and serve with mashed potatoes, rice, or pasta.

◆ *Serves 6*

Aromatic Lamb Kabobs

Souvlaki

Souvlaki is one of the most popular Greek dishes. You can also make souvlaki sandwiches on pita bread.

2½ to 3 pounds boneless lamb, cut into 1½-inch cubes

Oil, to brush grill
Lemon slices, for garnish

Marinade:

¼ cup olive oil

1 large onion, grated

3 cloves garlic, minced

2 bay leaves, crushed

1 teaspoon dried oregano

1 teaspoon dried thyme

1 teaspoon cumin

Juice of 1 lemon

½ cup dry red wine

Salt and freshly ground pepper

Rinse lamb cubes and put into a large bowl. In a medium bowl, combine oil, onion, garlic, bay leaves, oregano, thyme, cumin, lemon juice, wine, and salt and pepper to taste. Stir mixture, pour over the lamb, and turn to coat. Cover and marinade in refrigerator for 4 to 8 hours. Preheat and oil grill. Remove lamb cubes from marinade and thread 5 to 6 onto each metal skewer. Place skewers on oiled grill rack and cook, turning occasionally, for 10 to 15 minutes on each side, or until tender. Transfer to a large platter, garnish with lemon slices, and serve hot with rice pilaf, tzatziki, Greek salad, and warm pita bread.

◆ *Serves 4 to 5*

Aromatic Lamb with Tomato Sauce and Pasta

ARNAKI ME MACARONIA

This aromatic lamb dish is my mother's favorite dish for Sunday dinner.

3½ to 4 pounds lean leg of lamb or shoulder, cut into large stewing pieces

¼ cup olive oil

1 cup finely chopped onion

3 cloves garlic, finely chopped

½ cup red wine

1 cup peeled and chopped tomatoes

1 tablespoon tomato paste

1 cinnamon stick

1 bay leaf

Salt and pepper

2 cups water

1 pound spaghetti or any pasta

¾ cup grated kefalotyri or Parmesan cheese

In a medium saucepan, heat oil; add the meat and lightly brown on all sides. Add onion and garlic and sauté, stirring continuously, until lightly brown. Stir in wine, tomatoes, tomato paste, cinnamon, bay leaf, salt and pepper, and 2 cups of water. Cover and simmer for 1½ hours over medium heat, or until the meat is tender and sauce is thickened, adding more water if necessary. Cook pasta according to package directions. Drain, place on a warm platter, and sprinkle with half of the cheese. Remove cinnamon and bay leaf and spoon the lamb and sauce over pasta. Sprinkle with the rest of the cheese. Serve hot with a tossed salad, bread, and a glass of wine.

◆ *Serves 6*

Baked Lamb with Potatoes

Arni me Patates sto Fourno

This popular dish is served for Sunday dinners and holidays. Accompany it with Romaine lettuce salad, tzatziki sauce, and dry red wine.

1 leg of lamb (5 to 6 pounds), bone in or out

Juice of 3 lemons

Salt and pepper

1 tablespoon finely chopped fresh oregano

1½ tablespoons chopped fresh thyme

5 cloves garlic, peeled

1 tablespoon crushed garlic

¼ cup olive oil

2 cups water, divided

6 large potatoes, peeled, washed, and quartered

Lemon slices, for garnish

Preheat the oven to 350 degrees. Wash the lamb, trim all excess fat, and squeeze the juice of 2 lemons over it. Add salt and pepper to taste and sprinkle with half the oregano and thyme. With a sharp knife, make small slits all around the leg; insert whole cloves of garlic into the holes and rub the leg with half of the crushed garlic. Place lamb in a large baking pan, drizzle with olive oil, and add 1 cup of the water to the pan. Bake for 1 hour. Put potatoes in a large bowl and sprinkle them with juice of 1 lemon, salt and pepper to taste, and remaining oregano, thyme, and crushed garlic. Remove lamb from the oven and arrange the potatoes around it in the baking pan. Add 1 cup of water and bake for another 1½ hours to 2 hours, basting the lamb with its own juices. Remove pan from the oven and let stand for 5 minutes. Slice the meat and arrange on a large platter, surround with potatoes, and garnish with lemon slices.

◆ *Serves 8*

Corfu Spicy Veal Stew with Pasta

KERKIRAIKI PATSITSADA

This delicious dish can be served any night of the week; it's easy to make and goes well with a glass of dry red wine.

3 to 3½ pounds boneless beef or veal, cut into large stewing pieces

¼ cup olive oil

1 cup finely chopped onions

4 cloves garlic, finely chopped

1 cup white wine

3 cups chopped and peeled fresh tomatoes, with juice, or 1 (28-ounce) can peeled tomatoes, chopped, with juice

2 teaspoons tomato paste

1 teaspoon sugar

2 cinnamon sticks

2 whole cloves

2 bay leaves

Salt and freshly ground pepper

2 cups water

1 pound spaghetti or any pasta

¾ cup grated kefalotyri or Parmesan cheese

In a large pot, heat olive oil and sauté meat to brown lightly on all sides. Add onion and garlic and stir frequently for 5 minutes. Add wine, tomatoes, tomato paste, sugar, cinnamon, cloves, bay leaves, salt and pepper, and 2 cups of water. Cover and simmer over medium heat for about 2 hours, or until meat is tender and sauce is thickened, adding water if necessary. Cook pasta according to package directions. Drain and place pasta on a warm platter, top with meat and sauce, and sprinkle with cheese; serve hot.

◆ *Serves 6*

Delicious Pork Kabobs

Xirina Souvlakia

This is a delicious dinner to enjoy with family and friends.

3 to 3½ pounds lean pork, cut into 1½-inch cubes

Oil, to brush grill

2 medium green bell peppers, cut into 1½-inch squares

1 large onion, cut into 1½-inch squares

12 cherry tomatoes

Marinade:

¼ cup olive oil

Juice of 1 lemon

½ cup white wine

3 cloves garlic, minced

1 tablespoon chopped fresh oregano

1 teaspoon dried thyme

2 bay leaves, crushed

Salt and freshly ground pepper

Put the pork in a large bowl. To make marinade, combine oil, lemon juice, wine, garlic, oregano, thyme, bay leaves, and salt and pepper. Pour over the pork and stir to coat with marinade. Cover and refrigerate for 4 hours or up to 12 hours. Preheat and oil grill. Remove meat from marinade, reserving the liquid. Thread pork, peppers, onions, and tomatoes on metal skewers, leaving space between each piece. Cook, turning occasionally, for 12 to 15 minutes until pork is tender. Remove from the grill, arrange on a platter, and serve with rice pilaf, salad, and red wine.

◆ *Serves 5 to 6*

Delicious Pork with Leeks

HIRINO ME PRASA

¼ cup olive oil

½ cup finely chopped onion

½ cup chopped celery

3 cloves garlic, minced

3 to 3½ pounds lean boneless pork, cut into large stewing pieces

½ cup dry white wine

1½ cups tomatoes, peeled and chopped, with juice, or 1 cup canned crushed tomatoes

1 bay leaf

1 cinnamon stick

Salt and pepper

1½ cups water

2 large bunches of leeks, washed thoroughly and cut into 1-inch pieces

Chopped parsley, for garnish

In a large pot, heat the oil and sauté onion, celery, and garlic until soft; add pork and sauté for 10 minutes, or until lightly browned. Stir in wine, tomatoes with juice, bay leaf, cinnamon, and salt and pepper to taste. Add 1½ cups water, cover, and simmer over medium heat for 1 hour. Add leeks and more water if necessary and cook for 30 to 40 minutes, or until pork and leeks are tender and sauce is thickened. Remove from the heat, discard bay leaf and cinnamon stick, and sprinkle with chopped parsley. Serve this delicious dish with feta cheese on the side and white wine or retsina.

◆ *Serves 5 to 6*

Georgia's Roasted Leg of Lamb

ARNI PSITO STO FOURNO

Serve this dish with rice pilaf or roasted potatoes, tzatziki sauce, salad, and your favorite wine.

1 leg of lamb (5 to 6 pounds), boneless	2 tablespoons lemon juice
1½ teaspoons chopped fresh oregano	1 tablespoon olive oil
	Salt and pepper
	6 cloves garlic, peeled
1 tablespoon chopped fresh rosemary	1 cup water
	Rosemary sprigs, for garnish
1 tablespoon chopped fresh thyme	Lemon slices, for garnish

Wash and trim all excess fat off lamb and drain. In a small bowl, combine oregano, rosemary, thyme, lemon juice, oil, and salt and pepper to taste. Mix well. With a sharp knife make small slits all around the meat and insert some of the mixture into each slit, along with one whole garlic clove.

Marinade:

1 cup red wine	3 cloves garlic, crushed
Juice of 1 lemon	Salt and pepper
1 teaspoon oregano	

Place lamb in a large bowl. In a medium bowl, combine all ingredients and mix well. Pour marinade over lamb and turn to coat thoroughly. Cover and refrigerate for 6 hours or overnight. Preheat the oven to 350 degrees. Place leg of lamb in a large roasting pan and pour marinade over it and 1 cup of water into the bottom of the pan. Bake for about 2 to 2½ hours, or until lamb is tender and slightly rare. Baste every 20 to 25 minutes with pan juices and add more water if necessary. Remove from the oven and let stand for 5 minutes. Cut lamb and arrange slices on a large platter. Heat ½ cup of the remaining pan juices, pour over lamb slices, and garnish with fresh rosemary sprigs and lemon slices.

◆ *Serves 8*

Greek Lasagna

PASTITSIO

One of the most popular dishes in Greece is Greek lasagna. My sister Demitra can eat this dish everyday. Serve it with a side salad.

1 package pastitsio pasta (ziti or penne pasta may be substituted)

1 tablespoon salt

½ cup margarine

3 egg whites

2½ cups grated kefalotyri cheese

¼ cup olive oil plus additional for the pan

1 large onion, grated

3 cloves garlic, crushed

1 tablespoon chopped fresh mint

1 tablespoon chopped fresh basil

2½ pounds lean ground beef or lamb

½ cup white wine

1 cup crushed tomatoes

½ cup water

1 stick cinnamon

2 whole cloves

Salt and pepper

¼ cup dried bread crumbs

Georgia-Style Béchamel Sauce (see page 68)

Preheat the oven to 350 degrees. Fill a large pot with water; add 1 tablespoon salt and bring to a boil. Add pasta and boil for 10 minutes. Drain pasta and put it in a large bowl. Melt margarine in a small pan and pour over pasta. Lightly beat egg whites and pour over pasta. Using your hands, blend the pasta, egg whites, and ¾ cup of the cheese. Put ¼ cup oil in a medium saucepan and add onion, garlic, mint, and basil; sauté until tender. Add ground meat and sauté lightly, stirring constantly to break up the lumps. Slowly add wine, crushed tomatoes, ½ cup of water, cinnamon, cloves, and salt and pepper to taste. Simmer for 30 minutes, or until most of the water has evaporated. Remove the pan from the stove and mix in

½ cup cheese and the bread crumbs. Remove cinnamon stick and cloves and stir well. Prepare the béchamel sauce. Oil a 10 × 15 × 2½-inch baking pan and sprinkle the bottom with half the remaining cheese. Layer half the pasta mixture in the pan, spread the meat mixture on top of the pasta, and arrange the remaining pasta on top of the ground meat as before. Pour béchamel sauce over the top and sprinkle on the rest of the cheese. Bake for 1 hour. As soon as the top is golden brown, remove from the oven. Cool slightly before cutting.

♦ *Serves 8*

Note: Pastitsio macaroni is available at any Greek market.

Grilled Lamb Chops Stuffed with Feta Cheese

PAITHAKIA GEMISTA

This is the best treat! Try it and you'll love it!

2 to 3 pounds lamb chops, about 1 inch thick

Lemon slices, for garnish

Marinade:

¼ cup olive oil

Juice of 1 lemon

¼ cup white wine

3 cloves garlic, minced

1 teaspoon dried oregano

½ teaspoon dried thyme

1 bay leaf, crushed

Salt and pepper

Filling:

½ cup crumbled feta cheese

½ cup finely chopped red bell pepper

2 cloves garlic, minced

1 tablespoon finely chopped fresh flat parsley

1 tablespoon lemon juice

1 teaspoon olive oil

Freshly ground pepper

Wash lamb chops and pat dry. With a sharp knife, cut a horizontal pocket about 1½ inches wide in each lamb chop, from the meat side to the bone.

To make the marinade, in a medium bowl, stir together olive oil, lemon juice, wine, garlic, oregano, thyme, bay leaf, and salt and pepper. Pour marinade over chops, and turn to coat thoroughly. Cover and refrigerate for 3 to 6 hours.

To make the stuffing, combine feta, red pepper, garlic, parsley, lemon juice, olive oil, and pepper in a small bowl and mix well with a fork. Remove chops from marinade and drain, reserving the liquid. Preheat grill. Using a spoon, stuff lamb chops with the cheese filling and secure each with a toothpick. Place them on the grill and cook for about 10 to 12 minutes on each side for medium rare, or to your liking. Remove from grill, arrange chops on a platter, and garnish with lemon slices. Serve hot with rice pilaf and tomato and cucumber salad.

◆ *Serves 4*

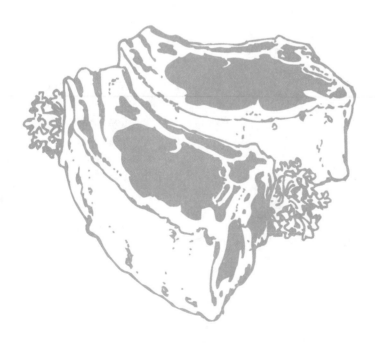

Grilled Lamb Chops with Mint Marinade

Arni Brizoles Sti Sxara me Diosmo

Serve these delicious lamb chops with tzatziki sauce, Greek salad, toasted bread, and a glass of retsina.

6 lamb or shoulder chops

Juice of 2 lemons

1½ tablespoons finely chopped fresh mint

3 cloves garlic, finely chopped

¼ cup olive oil

½ teaspoon dried oregano

½ teaspoon dried thyme

½ teaspoon nutmeg

1 teaspoon honey

Salt and freshly ground pepper

Lemon slices, for garnish

Mint sprigs, for garnish

In a large bowl, combine lemon juice, mint, garlic, oil, oregano, thyme, nutmeg, honey, and salt and pepper to taste; stir. Trim fat around chops, then wash them and pat dry. Wrap chops in plastic wrap and beat them with a meat tenderizer. Add chops to the marinade, then cover and refrigerate for at least for 4 hours or overnight. Preheat the grill. Remove chops from the marinade and place on grill rack 6 inches from the coals and cook for 8 to 10 minutes on each side until chops are tender. Arrange on a platter and garnish with lemon slices and mint sprigs.

◆ *Serves 3*

Grilled or Broiled Pork Chops

XIRINES BRIZOLES STI SXARA

4 to 5 large pork chops

Marinade:

½ cup dry white wine

2 tablespoons olive oil

3 cloves garlic, minced

1 tablespoon chopped fresh oregano

1 teaspoon honey

1 teaspoon finely chopped
   fresh thyme

1 bay leaf, crushed

Salt and freshly ground pepper

Trim excess fat from pork chops and place them in a large bowl. In a small bowl, combine wine, oil, garlic, oregano, honey, thyme, bay leaf, and salt and pepper. Pour marinade over chops and turn to coat both sides thoroughly. Cover and refrigerate for 3 hours. Preheat the grill or broiler. Remove chops from marinade and place on grill rack about 6 inches above the coals; grill for 10 to 12 minutes on each side, turning occasionally, or until chops are tender. Serve with rice pilaf and Greek tomato and cucumber salad.

◆ *Serves 4 to 5*

Hamburgers Pane

BIFTEKI PANE

My children love this dish with homemade fried potatoes; your children will, too!

1½ to 2 pounds extra-lean ground beef	1 large tomato, peeled, seeded, and chopped
1 tablespoon finely chopped fresh parsley	1¼ cups plain bread crumbs, divided
1 tablespoon finely chopped fresh mint	Salt and pepper
1 large onion, grated and drained	3 egg whites, lightly beaten
½ teaspoon dried oregano	Olive oil, for frying
2 cloves garlic, crushed	Parsley sprig, for garnish

In a large bowl, combine meat, parsley, mint, onion, oregano, garlic, tomatoes, ½ cup of the bread crumbs, and salt and pepper. Knead all ingredients together very well with your hands. Cover and refrigerate for 1 hour. Form mixture into 2-inch-wide patties. Dip each patty into lightly beaten egg whites, then coat with the remaining ¾ cup of bread crumbs; let stand for 10 minutes. In a large skillet, heat 1 inch of olive oil and fry patties on both sides until golden brown. Remove from the skillet and drain on paper towels. Arrange on a platter, garnish with sprig of parsley, and serve hot with homemade French fries and salad.

◆ *Serves 5 to 6*

Note: To bake the bifteki instead, brush a baking pan with oil and line up the patties 1 inch apart. Cook at 350 degrees for 35 to 40 minutes or until brown.

Hamburgers Stuffed with Feta Cheese

Bifteki me Feta

This is a unique and delicious Greek version of the classic hamburger.

1½ pounds lean ground beef

1 large onion, grated

3 cloves garlic, crushed

½ teaspoon dried mint

2 tablespoons finely chopped fresh
   flat parsley

½ cup plain bread crumbs

1 teaspoon dried oregano

Salt and pepper

½ pound feta cheese, sliced

5 hamburger buns

Olive oil, to brush buns

2 large tomatoes, sliced

1 red onion, sliced

1 tablespoon chopped parsley

In a large bowl, combine beef with onion, garlic, mint, parsley, bread crumbs, oregano, and salt and pepper to taste. Knead with hands to mix all ingredients. Cover and refrigerate for 1 hour. Preheat the grill. Divide meat mixture into 8 large flat patties, cover top of 4 patties with a slice of feta cheese, and top with remaining patties, pressing around the edges to seal well. Grill each patty for 6 to 7 minutes on each side for medium rare, or until desired doneness. Meanwhile, brush buns with olive oil, place on rack cut side down, and grill until golden brown. Place each burger on bottom half of toasted bun, top with tomato slice and onion slice, sprinkle with parsley, and cover with the top half of bun. Serve hot with home-made fried potatoes.

◆ *Serves 5*

Lamb Chops Pane

Arni Paithakia Pane

Serve hot, with fried zucchini or potatoes and salad.

6 to 8 lamb chops
4 leaves romaine lettuce

Lemon wedges, for garnish
Sprig fresh oregano, for garnish

Marinade:

¼ cup olive oil
Juice of 1 lemon
¼ cup dry red wine
3 cloves garlic, crushed

1 tablespoon chopped fresh oregano
½ teaspoon crushed dried rosemary
Salt and pepper

Batter:

1 egg
2 egg whites
1 cup flour

1 cup plain bread crumbs
¼ cup olive oil

Trim any excess fat from lamb chops; wash and pat dry. In a large bowl, mix oil, lemon, wine, garlic, oregano, rosemary, salt and pepper. Add lamb chops and turn to coat with the marinade, then cover and refrigerate for 6 to 8 hours. In a medium bowl, lightly beat egg and whites. Remove chops from the marinade and drain. Coat each lamb chop with flour, dip in egg mixture, then coat with bread crumbs. Allow chops to stand for 15 minutes. In a large skillet over medium heat, heat the olive oil, add the chops, and cook for 6 to 7 minutes per side. Remove from the skillet and drain excess oil on paper towels. Arrange lettuce leaves on a platter, top with lamb chops, and garnish with lemon wedges and a fresh sprig of oregano.

◆ *Serves 4*

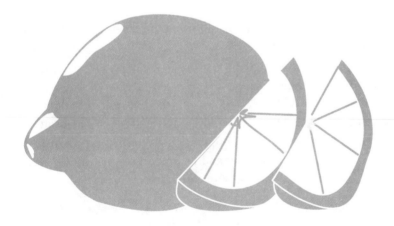

Lamb Ragout with Potatoes

Arni Kokinisto me Patates

1 leg of lamb (3 to 3½ pounds)	1 cinnamon stick
¼ cup olive oil	Salt and pepper
1 large onion, finely chopped	2 cups water
3 cloves garlic, chopped	2 pounds small white gourmet
½ cup dry red wine	potatoes, peeled, washed, and
1 cup canned crushed tomatoes	drained
1 teaspoon tomato paste	1 tablespoon chopped fresh parsley,
1 bay leaf	for garnish

Cut the meat into medium-size pieces; wash and pat dry. In a large saucepan, heat oil, then add the meat and lightly brown on both sides. Add onion and garlic and sauté for 5 minutes. Stir in wine, tomatoes, tomato paste, bay leaf, cinnamon, salt and pepper, and 2 cups of water. Cover and allow the meat to cook for 1½ hours, or until almost done. Add potatoes to the pot with the meat, along with more water if necessary and salt and pepper to taste. Continue cooking until meat and potatoes are ready and liquid absorbed. Remove from the heat and let stand for 5 minutes. Arrange the meat in the center of a platter, with the potatoes surrounding it; sprinkle with chopped parsley.

♦ *Serves 6*

Note: You can substitute beef or veal for the lamb in this dish.

Lamb with Spinach and Egg Lemon Sauce

Mosxari me Spanaki Avgolemono

This is a delicious dish when served with bread and a glass of wine.

3 to 3½ pounds boneless lamb

¼ cup olive oil

1 large onion, finely chopped

2 cups water

2 pounds fresh spinach

3 tablespoons finely chopped
  fresh parsley

3 tablespoon finely chopped
  fresh dill

Salt and pepper

Cut the lamb into portions; wash and pat dry. Heat oil in a large pot, add meat, and sauté until lightly brown. Add onions and sauté for 5 minutes. Add 2 cups of water, cover the pot, and simmer for 1½ hours, or until lamb is tender. Meanwhile, clean the spinach and cut each leaf into 2 or 3 pieces. Blanch in a pot of boiling water and drain in a colander. Remove the lamb from the pot and set aside temporarily. To the same pot in which the lamb was cooked, add spinach, parsley, dill, salt and pepper, and more water if necessary. Put the lamb on top of the spinach, cover the pot, and simmer for an additional 25 to 30 minutes over low heat, or until just a little sauce remains.

Egg lemon sauce:

2 eggs

Juice of 2 lemons

To make the sauce, beat 2 eggs in a medium bowl while slowly adding lemon juice. Ladle 1 cup of sauce from the pot slowly into the eggs as you beat them. Beat a little longer, then add the mixture to the lamb and spinach. Reduce heat to very low and simmer for 1 to 2 minutes; do not allow the mixture to boil.

◆ *Serves 6*

Lemon Garlic Roasted Pork Loin

HIRINO LATHORIGANO STO FOURNO

These lemon garlic pork loins are delicious with rice pilaf, tomato and cucumber salad, tzatziki sauce, and wine.

3½ to 4 pounds boneless center-cut pork loin

6 cloves garlic, peeled

1 tablespoon chopped fresh oregano

¼ cup olive oil

¼ cup white wine

Juice of 2 lemons

3 garlic cloves, minced

1 tablespoon chopped fresh thyme

1 bay leaf, crushed

Salt and pepper

1 cup water

Lemon slices, for garnish

Wash pork loin and pat dry. Then, with a sharp knife, make 6 slits in the pork loin and insert the whole garlic cloves and some fresh oregano into each one. Place in a large bowl. In a medium bowl, combine oil, wine, lemon juice, minced garlic, thyme, bay leaf, and salt and pepper and mix well. Pour marinade over the pork loin and turn to cover all sides. Cover and refrigerate for 6 hours or overnight. Preheat oven to 350 degrees. Place pork loin in a baking pan and add 1 cup of water. Bake for 1½ hours, or until pork loin is tender and juices are clear, basting occasionally with pan juices. Remove from the oven and let stand for 10 minutes. Slice the pork loin and arrange slices on a large platter. Pour some of the remaining juices over the pork and garnish with slices of lemon.

◆ *Serves 6*

Meatballs with Tomato Sauce

KEFTETHAKIA ME TOMATA

Serve these delicious meatballs with pasta or homemade fried potatoes.

4 slices Italian bread, crust
    removed, or ½ cup plain
    bread crumbs
1 pound lean ground beef or lamb
1 pound lean ground pork
1 large onion, grated
3 cloves garlic, minced
2 tablespoons finely chopped
    fresh parsley

2 tablespoons finely chopped
    fresh mint
1 teaspoon dried oregano
1 egg
Salt and pepper
Flour
Olive oil, for frying
Chopped parsley, for garnish

Tomato sauce:

2 tablespoons olive oil
1 medium onion, finely chopped
2 cloves garlic, finely chopped
1 can (28 ounces) crushed tomatoes

½ teaspoon sugar
1 cinnamon stick
Salt and pepper
¾ cup water

Soften bread in a little water and squeeze very dry. In large bowl, combine meats, onion, garlic, parsley, mint, oregano, softened bread or bread crumbs, egg, and salt and pepper. Knead until ingredients are well mixed. Cover and refrigerate for 1 hour. Make meatballs with 1 tablespoon of the mixture each and dredge them in flour. In a large skillet, heat 1 inch of olive oil until very hot and fry meatballs a few at a time, turning constantly, until golden brown. Drain on paper towels.

To prepare the sauce, in a medium saucepan, heat oil, sauté onion and garlic for 5 minutes, then stir in tomatoes, sugar, cinnamon, salt and pepper, and ¾ cup of water. Cook over low heat for about 30 minutes, or until sauce thickens. Arrange meatballs on a large platter and pour the sauce over them. Garnish with chopped parsley.

◆ *Serves 4 to 5*

Meat Loaf with Feta Cheese

Rolo me Gemisto me Feta

1 pound extra-lean ground beef

1 pound extra-lean ground pork

1 egg

1 large onion, grated

3 cloves garlic, minced

2 tablespoons chopped fresh
　flat parsley

1 medium red bell pepper, finely
　chopped

1 teaspoon dried oregano

½ teaspoon ground cumin

1 teaspoon ground cinnamon

2 cups soft bread crumbs

Salt and pepper

½ pound feta cheese, cut into
　½-inch slices

1 tablespoon olive oil, plus extra
　to oil baking pan

1 cup water

In a large bowl, combine beef, pork, egg, onion, garlic, parsley, red pepper, oregano, cumin, cinnamon, bread crumbs, and salt and pepper. Mix well, cover, and refrigerate for 1 hour. Preheat the oven to 350 degrees. Flour a flat surface and spread meat mixture onto surface in an oval shape. Place feta slices lengthwise in the middle of the meat mixture, then fold the meat over the cheese and shape into a cylinder. Place the roll in the center of an oiled baking pan, add 1 cup of water to the pan, drizzle with 1 tablespoon olive oil, and bake for 1½ hours. Remove from the oven and let stand for 10 minutes, then slice and serve with crusty bread and tomato and cucumber salad.

◆ *Serves 6*

Meat Loaf Roll Stuffed with Eggs

ROLO GEMISTO ME AUGA

This meat loaf dish is delicious, with stuffed eggs!

3 eggs, hard-boiled

2½ pounds lean ground beef or
    lamb

1 raw egg

1 large onion, grated

¼ cup finely chopped fresh parsley

2 tablespoons finely chopped
    fresh mint

1 tablespoon dried oregano

3 cloves garlic, crushed

½ teaspoon allspice

¾ cup dry bread crumbs

Salt and pepper

¼ cup olive oil, plus extra to oil
    baking pan

1 cup water

Preheat the oven to 350 degrees. Peel hard-boiled eggs and set aside. Put the meat and raw egg in a large bowl. Add onion, parsley, mint, oregano, garlic, allspice, breadcrumbs, and salt and pepper to taste. Knead until well blended. Flour a flat surface and spread meat mixture onto surface in an oval shape. Place the hard-boiled eggs lengthwise (vertically) in the middle of meat mixture. Fold the meat over the eggs and shape into a cylinder. Oil a 9 × 13 × ½-inch baking pan, place the roll in the center, add 1 cup of water, and bake for about 1½ hours. Remove from the oven and cool for 15 minutes before slicing.

◆ *Serves 6*

Moussaka

MOUSSAKA

Moussaka is very popular in Greece among natives and tourists. This delicious dish consists of eggplant, ground meat, and a creamy béchamel sauce. Serve it with Greek salad and dry red or white wine.

4 large eggplants
1 cup olive oil or more, for frying
   eggplants

Meat sauce:

¼ cup olive oil
1 large onion, finely chopped
3 cloves garlic, finely chopped
¼ cup finely chopped fresh parsley
2 tablespoons chopped fresh mint
2 tablespoons finely chopped fresh
   basil or 1 teaspoon dried basil
2½ pounds ground beef
¼ cup red dry wine
1 teaspoon ground cinnamon

Salt and pepper
1½ cups peeled and crushed
   tomatoes or 1 can (16 ounces)
   whole tomatoes, crushed,
   with juice
¼ cup dry bread crumbs
¾ cup grated kefalotyri cheese
Georgia-Style Béchamel Sauce
   (see page 68)

Peel and wash eggplant, then slice lengthwise into 1-inch slices. Put eggplant slices in a colander, sprinkle with salt, and let sit for 1 hour. Rinse eggplant, place on paper towels, and pat dry. In a large skillet, heat the oil and fry eggplant on both sides until lightly browned. Drain on paper towels and set aside. To make the sauce, heat olive oil in a medium saucepan and add onion, garlic, parsley, mint, and basil and sauté for 5 minutes. Add ground meat and sauté until barely brown. Add wine, stirring continuously to break up any lumps. Stir in cinnamon, salt and pepper to taste, and crushed tomatoes with juice. Cover and simmer over medium heat for 30 minutes or until liquid has been absorbed. Remove from the stove and cool for 5 minutes. Add bread crumbs and ½ cup cheese to meat sauce and mix well. Prepare béchamel sauce. Arrange half of the eggplant slices on the bottom of a 10 × 15-inch baking pan, sprinkle with ¼ cup of cheese, and cover with an even layer of the meat mixture. Layer remaining eggplant slices on top of the meat, then spread béchamel sauce over the top and bake until golden brown. Remove from the oven and cool for 20 minutes before cutting.

◆ *Serves 6*

Oven-Baked Lamb with Zucchini

ARNI STO FOURNO ME KOLOKITHAKIA

This dish is delicious during summer, with fresh garden zucchini.

3½ to 4 pounds lean boneless lamb, cut into large pieces

¼ cup olive oil

1 large onion, finely chopped

3 cloves garlic, finely chopped

1½ tablespoons finely chopped fresh mint

2 tablespoons chopped fresh flat parsley

½ cup dry red wine

2 cups fresh tomatoes, peeled and chopped, with juice

Salt and pepper, to taste

1 cup water

¼ cup olive oil

6 to 7 very small zucchini, cut in half and stems removed

Preheat the oven to 350 degrees. Wash lamb pieces and pat them dry. Heat oil in a large skillet and lightly brown the lamb. Add onion, garlic, mint, and parsley and stir for 7 to 8 minutes. Stir in wine, then remove skillet from the heat. Place lamb mixture in a large baking pan and add chopped tomatoes, salt and pepper to taste, and 1 cup of water. Cover with foil and bake for 1 hour. Meanwhile heat ¼ cup of oil in large skillet, add zucchini a few pieces at a time, and lightly brown on both sides; drain on paper towels. Remove baking pan from the oven, arrange zucchini around the lamb, and baste with pan juices. Add more water if necessary and continue baking, uncovered, for another 40 to 45 minutes, or until lamb and zucchini are tender and most of the water has evaporated. Remove from the oven and let stand for 5 minutes; serve hot. This is my favorite dish; it's great with salad and warm crusty bread.

◆ *Serves 4 to 5*

Pork Fricassee

Xirino Fricase

3 pounds boneless pork, cut into
    large pieces for stewing
¼ cup olive oil
1 cup chopped scallions
1 large onion, chopped
3 cups water, divided
Salt and pepper to taste

1 large head romaine lettuce,
    washed and outer leaves
    discarded
¼ cup chopped fresh dill
¼ cup chopped fresh parsley
2 eggs
Juice of 1 lemon

Wash and drain pork, then brown lightly in olive oil in a medium pot. Add scallions and onion and stir 5 to 6 minutes, then add 2 cups of the water and salt and pepper to taste and bring to a slow boil. Simmer for about 1 hour. Cut each lettuce leaf into 3 or 4 pieces and toss in a large bowl with dill and parsley. Add to the pork, along with 1 cup water. Bring to a boil and simmer for 45 minutes, until pork and lettuce are cooked through. In a small bowl, beat eggs, add lemon juice, and blend thoroughly. Slowly add 1 cup of liquid from the pot to the eggs, while continuing to blend. Beat for 2 to 3 minutes. Slowly add this mixture to the pot of meat, stirring continuously. Remove the pot from the stove and serve hot.

◆ *Serves 6*

Roasted Pork with Potatoes

XIRINO PSITO ME PATATES

If you're looking for a dish to treat your family or guests, you have to try this.

4 to 4½ pounds pork loin

5 to 6 cloves garlic, peeled

Lemon slices, for garnish

Lemon marinade:

Juice of 2 lemons

¼ cup olive oil

1 teaspoon dried oregano

1 tablespoon chopped fresh thyme

2 cloves garlic, minced

Salt and pepper

5 to 6 large baking potatoes,
   peeled, washed, and quartered

1 teaspoon paprika

1 cup water

Trim excess fat from the pork; wash and pat dry. With a sharp knife make small slits all over the pork and insert garlic cloves. Place in a large bowl. To make the marinade, combine lemon juice, oil, oregano, thyme, garlic, and salt and pepper in a small jar and mix well. Pour marinade over the pork and turn to coat. Cover and refrigerate for 4 to 6 hours. Preheat the oven to 350 degrees. Place pork in a large baking pan and arrange potatoes around it. Pour marinade over the pork and potatoes and season with more salt and pepper to taste and paprika. Add 1 cup water and bake for 1½ to 2 hours, or until pork and potatoes turn brown, adding more water if necessary and basting with pan juices. Remove from the oven and let stand for 10 minutes. Slice the pork, arrange on a platter, and surround with potatoes. Garnish with lemon slices and serve with Greek salad.

◆ *Serves 6*

Roast pork with potatoes.

Roasted Rack of Lamb with Lemon

PAITHAKIA ARNI STO FOURNO

This dish is easy to prepare and delicious with a nice glass of wine.

1 rack of lamb with 8 chops	½ teaspoon dried thyme
¼ cup olive oil	Juice of 2 lemons
4 cloves garlic, minced	2 bay leaves, crushed
1 tablespoon chopped fresh oregano	Salt and pepper
1 teaspoon chopped fresh rosemary	Lemon slices, for garnish

Wash the lamb, pat dry, place in a large bowl. In a small bowl, combine oil, garlic, oregano, rosemary, thyme, lemon juice, bay leaves, and salt and pepper and mix well. Pour marinade over the lamb and turn to coat. Cover and refrigerate for 6 hours. Preheat the oven to 350 degrees. Roast lamb with marinade for 1½ hours, or until cooked to your preference, basting often and adding a little water to the pan if necessary. Remove from the oven and let stand for 10 minutes. Cut into individual chops and serve on a platter with lemon slices. This dish is great with rice and salad.

♦ *Serves 4*

Sausage with Peppers and Onions

Loukaniko me Pipergies kai Kremidia

This special dish is from the Pelion region in Thessaly, Greece.

1 to 1½ pounds Greek loukaniko
   or fresh Italian pork sausage
¼ cup olive oil
1 large red bell pepper, sliced into
   long strips
1 large green bell pepper, sliced
   into long strips
2 medium onions, sliced

3 cloves garlic, chopped
3 medium ripe tomatoes, peeled
   and chopped, with juice
½ cup water
1 teaspoon dried oregano
1 teaspoon dried thyme
1 bay leaf
Salt and pepper

Cut sausage into 1-inch pieces and brown lightly on all sides; remove and drain on paper towels. In a large skillet, heat olive oil and sauté peppers, onions, and garlic for 6 to 7 minutes, stirring continuously. Add tomatoes, ½ cup of water, oregano, thyme, bay leaf, and salt and pepper to taste and cook for 10 minutes. Stir in sausage, reduce heat to low, and simmer, covered, for 30 minutes, adding more water if necessary. Remove from heat and serve hot with plenty of crusty bread and wine.

◆ *Serves 4 to 5*

Spiced Pork with Cabbage in Tomato Sauce

HIRINO ME DOMATA

This is a delicious dish by itself or with bread and a glass of dry white wine.

2½ to 3 pounds pork, cut into
    large stewing pieces
¼ cup olive oil
1 large onion, finely chopped
½ cup chopped celery
3 cloves garlic, chopped
1 can (28 ounces) whole plum
    tomatoes, chopped, with juice

2 cups water
1 cinnamon stick
2 bay leaves
1 medium head cabbage (2 to 2½
    pounds), washed, any yellow
    leaves removed, cored,
    and sliced
Salt and freshly ground pepper

Wash the pork and pat dry. In a large pot, heat the oil and sauté pork until lightly browned on all sides. Add onion, celery, and garlic and stir for 5 to 6 minutes. Add tomatoes, 2 cups of water, cinnamon, and bay leaves. Cover the pot and simmer over medium heat for 50 minutes to 1 hour. Blanch sliced cabbage in a large pot of boiling water and drain well. Stir cabbage into the pork, along with salt and pepper to taste, adding more water if necessary. Cover and simmer over low heat for 40 minutes, or until meat and cabbage are tender and most of the water has evaporated. Remove from the heat and let stand for 5 minutes. Remove cinnamon stick and bay leaves and serve hot with plenty of bread and feta cheese.

◆ *Serves 6*

Stove-Top Roasted Lamb with Lemon

ARNI LATHORIGANO

T his excellent dish is one of my mother's and very easy to make; my
son Peter loves it. You can use pork instead of lamb, if you prefer.

3 to 3 ½ pounds lean lamb
   (e.g., lamb shoulder), cut into
   large pieces
¼ cup olive oil
4 cloves garlic, minced
1 teaspoon dried oregano
1½ teaspoons chopped fresh thyme

Juice of 2 lemons
1 bay leaf
1 cup water
Salt and pepper
Lemon slices, for garnish
Fresh thyme, for garnish

Wash and trim excess fat from lamb and pat dry. Heat oil in a large pot and
brown lamb on all sides. Add garlic and cook, stirring, for 1 minute. Stir in
oregano, thyme, and lemon juice and cook for 5 minutes, then add bay leaf,
water, and salt and pepper to taste. Cover and simmer for 1 hour and 20
minutes, or until meat is tender. Add more water during the cooking
process if necessary, but allow most of the liquid to evaporate, leaving just
a little oil and lemon. Remove from the stove and let stand for 5 minutes.
Arrange on a platter, garnish with lemon slices, and sprinkle with fresh
thyme. Serve with roasted potatoes or rice pilaf and tzatziki sauce.

♦ *Serves 4 to 5*

Stuffed Cabbage with Egg Lemon Sauce

DOLMADES AVGOLEMONO

These stuffed dolmades are delicious with creamy egg lemon sauce, crusty bread, and your favorite wine.

1 large head cabbage (3½ to 4 pounds)	¼ cup finely chopped fresh parsley
2 pounds ground beef	½ cup finely chopped fresh dill
½ cup uncooked long-grain white rice	3 eggs
1 large onion, finely chopped	Salt and pepper
	¼ cup olive oil
	Juice of 1 or 2 lemons

Remove cabbage stem and blanch in a large pot of boiling water for 25 to 30 minutes; set aside to drain and cool. When cabbage is cool enough to handle, remove leaves, one by one, and set aside to cool. In a large bowl, mix beef, rice, onion, parsley, dill, 1 egg, and salt and pepper; knead well. Place 1½ tablespoons of meat mixture near the base of each cabbage leaf, fold in the sides, and roll it up. Place stuffed cabbage rolls open side down in a large pot and sprinkle with salt and pepper to taste. Pour olive oil over the rolls, add enough water to cover, and place a plate on top. Simmer over medium heat for 1 hour, or until cooked and about 1 cup of sauce remains. To make the sauce, mix 2 eggs and lemon juice in a blender for 2 minutes, slowly adding 1 cup of liquid from the pot while continuing to blend for another 2 minutes. Pour egg mixture over the rolls in the pot, reduce the heat, and simmer 2 minutes; do not allow to boil, and do not stir. Serve hot.

◆ *Serves 6*

Stuffed Grape Leaves with Egg Lemon Sauce

Dolmadakia Avgolemono

This delicious dish can be served as a main course or without the egg lemon sauce as an appetizer.

1½ to 2 pounds ground beef

1 large onion, grated

¼ cup finely chopped fresh parsley

3 tablespoons finely chopped
   fresh dill

½ cup cooked long-grain white rice

2 tablespoons finely chopped
   fresh mint

1 egg, beaten

Salt and pepper to taste

2 tablespoons olive oil

1 jar (16 ounces) grape leaves

In a large bowl, combine beef, onion, parsley, dill, rice, mint, beaten egg, and salt and pepper; knead well to mix. Set aside for 15 minutes. Rinse and drain grape leaves and trim tough stems. Cover the bottom of a medium saucepan with 5 large leaves. Put 1 teaspoon of stuffing at the base of each remaining leaf, fold in the sides, and roll up. Place rolls close together in layers in the saucepan. Season with salt and pepper to taste. Drizzle with olive oil and add enough water to cover. Place a plate over the rolls, cover the pan, and simmer for 1 hour until the rolls are tender and the water has evaporated.

Egg lemon sauce:

2 cups chicken stock

2 eggs

Juice of 1 to 2 lemons

1 teaspoon cornstarch

Pinch of salt

Boil stock in a small saucepan. Meanwhile, in a blender, beat the eggs and slowly add lemon juice, cornstarch, and salt, then, with machine running slowly, add 1 cup hot stock. Stir egg mixture into hot stock and cook over low heat until thickened; do not allow to come to a boil. Pour egg lemon sauce over the rolls, but do not stir. Remove from heat, let stand for 10 minutes, and serve. The creamy egg lemon sauce makes this a delicious dish. Serve with bread and a glass of wine.

♦ *Serves 6*

Stuffed Leg of Lamb with Ham and Cheese

Arni Gemisto me Zambon

This recipe is elegant and easy to prepare for any occasion.

1 boneless leg of lamb
    (5 to 6 pounds)
Juice of 1 lemon
Salt and pepper
3 cloves garlic, minced
1 teaspoon dried oregano
6 slices ham

1 cup kefalotyri cheese cut into
    small cubes (Romano pecorino
    cheese can be substituted for
    kefalotyri)
5 to 6 cloves garlic, peeled
1 cup water

Trim excess fat from lamb; wash and pat dry. Open lamb so it lies flat and pound it lightly to create a flat surface for stuffing. Sprinkle with lemon juice, salt and pepper, garlic, and oregano, then top with ham slices and sprinkle cheese over the ham. Roll up the lamb and tie in several places with string to secure. With a sharp knife, make small slits all around the lamb and insert whole cloves of garlic.

Marinade:

¼ cup olive oil
1½ teaspoons dried oregano
2 bay leaves, crushed
½ teaspoon dried rosemary

Juice of 2 lemons
1 cup red wine
Salt and freshly ground pepper

To make the marinade, in a large bowl, mix oil, oregano, bay leaves, rosemary, lemon juice, red wine, and salt and pepper well. Put lamb in marinade and turn to coat. Cover and refrigerate for 3 hours, turning the lamb every 30 minutes.

Preheat the oven to 350 degrees. Place lamb into a roasting pan and pour marinade over it. Add 1 cup water to the bottom of the pan and bake for 2 to 2½ hours, baste with pan juices every 25 to 30 minutes, and add more water if necessary. Remove from the oven; let stand for 10 minutes. Slice lamb, arrange on a platter, and pour some hot pan juices over it. Serve with roasted potatoes or rice pilaf, tzatziki sauce, and salad.

◆ *Serves 6 to 8*

Stuffed Romaine Lettuce with Egg and Lemon Sauce

DOLMATHES ME MAROULI AVGOLEMONO

This is the best dish! The flavor of the lettuce makes a delicious marriage with the creamy egg lemon sauce.

1½ to 2 pounds extra-lean
    ground beef
1 large onion, grated
2 tablespoons chopped fresh flat
    parsley
2 tablespoons chopped fresh dill
½ cup uncooked long-grain
    white rice

1 egg
1 teaspoon dried mint
Salt and pepper
2 large heads romaine lettuce
2 tablespoons olive oil

Egg lemon sauce:

1½ to 2 cups chicken broth
2 eggs

Juice of 2 lemons

In a large bowl, combine meat, onion, parsley, dill, rice, egg, mint, and salt and pepper, then knead mixture well. Cover and refrigerate for 30 minutes. Clean the lettuce, discarding the tough outer leaves and stems. Blanch lettuce leaves briefly in boiling water and set aside to cool and drain. Take a lettuce leaf, place 1 tablespoon of stuffing near the base, fold in the sides, and roll up. Repeat with all the leaves, cutting in half any that are extra large. Place stuffed rolls open side down in a large pot, dribble olive oil over them, and sprinkle with salt and pepper to taste. Add water to cover the rolls and put a plate on top of the rolls. Cover the pot and simmer over medium heat for 1 hour, or until tender and most of the water has evaporated.

To make the sauce, bring the chicken broth to a boil in a small saucepan. Meanwhile, in a blender, beat eggs and lemon juice for 2 to 3 minutes, then slowly add the hot chicken broth to the egg mixture while blending. Pour the egg mixture over the rolls in the pot. Reduce heat to very low and simmer for 3 minutes, but do not allow the pot to boil and do not stir. Remove from heat and let stand for 10 minutes. Serve hot with bread and feta cheese.

◆ *Serves 6*

Veal Stew with Rice Pilaf

MOSXARAKI ME RIZI

This dish is heaven; serve it with crusty bread, tossed salad, and wine.

2½ to 3 pounds veal, cut into
    stewing pieces
¼ cup olive oil
1 cup finely chopped onion
3 cloves garlic, minced
½ cup white wine
1 pound ripe tomatoes, skinned
    and crushed, or 1½ cups canned
    crushed tomatoes

1 teaspoon sugar
1 stick cinnamon
Salt and freshly ground pepper
2 cups water
1-pound package uncooked
    rice pilaf
½ cup grated kefalotyri or
    Parmesan cheese

Wash veal pieces and pat dry. In a large saucepan, heat olive oil and sauté meat, stirring, until lightly brown on all sides. Stir in onion and garlic and sauté for 5 minutes. Add wine, tomatoes, sugar, cinnamon, salt and pepper, and 2 cups of water. Cover and cook over medium heat about 1½ hours, or until meat is tender and sauce is thickened, stirring from to time and adding water if necessary. Meanwhile, cook rice pilaf according to package directions. Place rice on a platter, sprinkle with half the cheese, then cover rice with the veal and sauce and sprinkle with remaining cheese. Serve hot.

♦ *Serves 5 to 6*

THE OLYMPIC GAMES:
A TIME TO CELEBRATE GREECE

*T*he enduring ideals of sport and fitness, noble competition, peace, and the inseparable nature of mind and body have been at the heart of the Olympics since the original games in 776 BCE. These ideals sparked the renewal of the modern games in 1896—also held in Greece—and will animate the games again.

The ancient games were held on the plains of Olympia on the coast of Peloponnese, near Athens. The site at Olympia included the original Olympic Stadium, a gymnasium, a dining hall, guest houses for high priests and athletes, the Altar of Oaths, where the athletes swore to abide by the rules of the Games, and many other buildings devoted to the gods. The stadium, built of marble, could seat forty-five thousand to fifty thousand people, but no one knows if it was ever full. The Games were celebrated continuously at Olympia for 1,100 years until they were banned in 393 CE. The buildings were burned down, and in the sixth century, an earthquake and flood buried the site under layers of mud. It wasn't until 1875 that excavation began to uncover this ancient site.

The site at Olympia has now been preserved. Visiting these ancient ruins is like going back in time—you can close your eyes and hear the roar of the crowd and see the glitter of priestly robes, the jewels on high officials, the athletes making history. The Olympia Museum, near the site, displays statuary, pots, tools, and ornaments that were uncovered during the excavation of Olympia.

Reflecting the values at the heart of the Olympics are the Olympic rings, the Olympic flame, the Olympic oath, creed, and motto, and the Olympic flag. The five interlocked Olympic rings represent unity among the five continents. The blue ring symbolizes Europe; the yellow ring, Asia; the black ring, Africa; the green ring, Australia; and the red ring, the Americas. On the Olympic flag, the five rings are set on a white background, which represents peace.

A tradition from ancient Greece, the Olympic flame is a symbol of purity, the struggle for victory, the pursuit of perfection, peace, and friendship. As in ancient times, the sun ignites the torch on the plains of Olympia, and it is passed from runner to runner until it reaches the host city.

According to Baron Pierre de Coubertin, founder of the modern Olympics, the Olympic creed best embodies what the games are all about: "The most important thing in the Olympic Games is not to win but to take part, just as the most important thing in life is not the triumph but the struggle. The essential thing is not to have conquered but to have fought well."

Perhaps the most important thing about Olympia is that it is thirty minutes from my childhood home in Peloponnese, and the Olympia Museum was the site of my memorable fifth-grade field trip. The ancient ruins at Olympia and the Olympic games have been part of my life since early childhood. The return of the games to Greece in 2004 is a time of celebration for me, a time to celebrate with Greek cuisine and a new cookbook.

The Parthenon in Athens, Greece.

Seafood Dishes

- Baked Fish Spetsiota   180
- Baked Fish Steaks with Potatoes and Onions   181
- Baked Fish with Peppers and Feta Cheese   182
- Fried Fish   184
- Fried Salted Cod   185
- Georgia's Stuffed Haddock   186
- Grilled Salmon   187
- Grilled Sardines with Garlic and Lemon Sauce   188
- Grilled Sardines with Grape Leaves   189
- Grilled Seafood Kabobs   190
- Grilled Swordfish Kabobs with Bay Leaves   192
- Lemon Fried Red Mullet   193
- Lemon Grilled Lobster Tails   194
- Marinated Baked Mackerel   195
- Mykonos Grilled Shrimp Souvlaki   196
- Shrimp Saganaki with Feta Cheese   197
- Shrimp with Ouzo   198
- Stuffed Squid with Rice   199

Baked Fish Spetsiota

Psari sto Fourno Spetsiotiko

This dish is originally from the island of Spetses in the Peloponnese region.

2 to 2½ pounds any fish fillets or whole fish (red snapper or sea bream)

¼ cup olive oil

2 cups fresh tomatoes, peeled and chopped, with juice

4 cloves garlic, finely chopped

2 large onions, thinly sliced

2 tablespoons chopped fresh flat parsley

1 tablespoon chopped fresh mint

¼ cup white wine

1 tablespoon chopped fresh basil

½ teaspoon dried oregano

Salt and pepper

Preheat the oven to 350 degrees. Wash and drain the fish. In a large bowl, combine olive oil, tomatoes, garlic, onion, parsley, mint, wine, basil, oregano, and salt and pepper and mix well. Place half this mixture in a baking pan, add the fish, then top with the remaining mixture. Bake for 1 hour, or until fish is tender and golden brown on top. Serve with skordalia (page 29) or salad. This dish is delicious and easy.

◆ *Serves 4 to 5*

Baked Fish Steaks with Potatoes and Onions

PSARI STO FOURNO ME PATATES

2 to 2½ pounds swordfish, halibut,
   or sea bass

Salt and pepper

2 large onions, thinly sliced

4 to 5 medium potatoes, peeled
   and cut into long narrow pieces

4 cloves garlic, thinly sliced

1½ tablespoons finely chopped
   fresh oregano

3 tablespoons olive oil

Juice of 1 lemon

¼ cup white wine

¾ cup water

Chopped parsley, for garnish

Preheat the oven to 350 degrees. Rinse the fish, pat dry, and season with salt and pepper. Spread onion slices in a large round baking pan. Place fish in the middle and surround with potato pieces. Sprinkle with garlic, oregano, olive oil, lemon juice, and salt and pepper to taste. Add wine and water and bake for about 1 hour, or until fish and potatoes are cooked, adding a little water if needed during cooking. Remove from the oven and let stand for 5 minutes. Serve fish on a platter surrounded by the onions and potatoes and sprinkle with chopped parsley. Pair this dish with steamed greens or salad.

♦ *Serves 4 to 5*

Baked Fish with Peppers and Feta Cheese

Psari sto Fourno me Pipergies kai Feta

This delicious fish dish is a perfect meal.

1½ to 2 pounds fish fillets (haddock or cod), skin removed
Salt
Juice of 1 lemon
¼ cup olive oil
1 large onion, sliced
1 large red bell pepper, sliced into strips
1 large green bell pepper, sliced into strips
1 large yellow bell pepper, sliced into strips

3 cloves garlic, crushed
2 medium fresh tomatoes, peeled and sliced
¼ cup white wine
1 tablespoon chopped fresh mint
1 tablespoon chopped fresh flat parsley
Salt and pepper
½ pound feta cheese, cut into slices
Chopped parsley or mint, for garnish

Preheat the oven 350 degrees. Wash fish, pat dry, and cut into 6-ounce pieces. Sprinkle with salt and lemon juice, set aside. In a large skillet, heat oil and sauté onion for 2 minutes. Add pepper strips and garlic and sauté for 5 to 6 minutes. Stir in tomatoes, wine, mint, parsley, and salt and pepper to taste. Reduce heat to medium and simmer for 15 minutes, or until all the liquids have evaporated. Remove from the heat and cool slightly. Place fish in a baking pan, spoon the pepper mixture evenly on each fish piece, then top each one with a slice of feta. Spoon any remain pepper mixture around the pan and bake for 35 to 40 minutes, or until golden. Serve hot with rice pilaf and garnish with parsley or mint.

◆ *Serves 4 to 5*

Fried Fish

Tiganito Psari

1½ to 2 pounds haddock, cod, or fillet of sole	1 egg
Salt	1 cup milk
Juice of 1 lemon	Olive oil, for frying
1 cup flour	Lemon slices, for garnish
½ cup corn flour	Parsley, for garnish

Wash fish, pat dry, and cut into 6-ounce pieces. Put on a large platter and sprinkle with salt to taste and juice of 1 lemon. Let stand in the refrigerator for 30 minutes. Mix flours. In a medium bowl, beat eggs and milk for 2 minutes. Dip fish in the egg mixture, then into flour, shaking off any excess. In a large skillet, heat 1 inch oil until very hot. Add 2 to 3 pieces of fish and fry 5 to 6 minutes on each side until golden brown. Remove fish and drain on paper towels. Arrange fish on a large platter, top with lemon slices, and garnish with parsley. Serve hot.

♦ *Serves 5 to 6*

Fried Salted Cod

BAKALIARO TIGANITO

This is another delicacy from the Greek table, served with skordalia.

1½ to 2 pounds dried salt cod
  fillets, cut into 3-inch squares

1 cup flour

½ cup corn flour

Pepper

1½ cups milk

1 large egg

Olive oil, for frying

1 to 2 fresh lemons

Lemon wedges, for garnish

Skordalia (page 25)

Soak the salt cod (bakaliaro) in enough cold water to cover, cover the pan, and refrigerate for 24 hours, changing the water at least five times to remove the salt. Before frying, remove salt cod from the water and drain. In a medium bowl, mix flours and pepper. In another bowl, beat milk and egg for 2 minutes. Dip fish pieces in egg mixture, then into the flour, shaking to remove any excess. In a large skillet, heat 2 inches of oil until very hot. Add 3 to 4 pieces of fish and fry for 5 minutes on each side, or until golden brown and crisp. Remove fish and drain on paper towels. Squeeze fresh lemon juice over the fish and garnish with lemon wedges. Serve hot with skordalia, salad, and white wine. Delicious!

◆ *Serves 4 to 5*

Georgia's Stuffed Haddock

PSARI YEMISTO

I used to serve this dish in my restaurant; the stuffing makes it elegant.

1½ to 2 pounds haddock or other
    fish fillets
Juice of 1 lemon
Salt and pepper
2 cups chopped and crumbled
    imitation crabmeat
3 cloves garlic, minced
2 tablespoons chopped fresh flat
    parsley
1 tablespoon chopped fresh mint

¼ cup plain bread crumbs
2 tablespoons olive oil, plus extra
    to brush baking pan and fish
1 teaspoon dried oregano
3 tablespoons grated Parmesan
    cheese
Paprika
Chopped parsley, for garnish
Lemon slices, for garnish

Preheat the oven to 350 degrees. Wash and pat the fish dry and cut into 6-ounce pieces. Place on a platter and sprinkle with lemon juice and salt and pepper on both sides. In large bowl, combine imitation crabmeat, garlic, parsley, mint, bread crumbs, olive oil, oregano, Parmesan cheese, and salt and pepper and mix well. Brush a 9 × 13 × 2½-inch baking pan with oil, put fish pieces in the pan, and brush the tops with oil. Top each piece of fish with enough stuffing to cover and sprinkle with paprika. Bake for 45 to 50 minutes, or until fish is tender and crisp on top. Remove from the oven, arrange on a platter, and garnish with chopped parsley and lemon slices. Serve this delicious dish with potato salad or any greens.

◆ *Serves 4*

Grilled Salmon

Solomos sta Karvouna

This is an easy and delicious recipe; serve with salad or any greens.

3 salmon steaks, cut into
   6-ounce pieces
3 tablespoons olive oil, plus extra
   to oil grill
Juice of 1 lemon
¼ cup white wine

1 tablespoon chopped fresh
   oregano
2 cloves garlic, crushed
½ teaspoon paprika
Salt and pepper

Wash salmon, pat dry, and place in a shallow dish. Combine olive oil, lemon juice, wine, oregano, garlic, paprika, and salt and pepper and mix well. Pour the marinade over the salmon, turn to coat, cover, and refrigerate for 3 hours. Preheat the grill, lightly oil it, and cook the salmon for 8 to 10 minutes on each side.

◆ *Serves 3*

Grilled Sardines with Garlic and Lemon Sauce

Sardeles sta Karvouna me Skordolemono

1 to 1½ pounds fresh sardines,
   heads removed, cleaned, rinsed
   with cold water, and drained

Salt and pepper
Lemon slices, for garnish

Place sardines in a bowl and sprinkle with salt and pepper.

Garlic lemon sauce:

¼ cup olive oil, plus extra to
   brush grill
Juice of 1½ lemons

3 cloves garlic, minced
1 teaspoon chopped fresh oregano
Salt and pepper

Preheat the grill and brush with oil. Grill sardines for 8 to 10 minutes on each side, turning once, or until fish is opaque. Remove to a large platter. In a medium bowl, combine oil, lemon juice, garlic, oregano, and salt and pepper and whisk well. Pour sauce on top of the sardines and garnish with the lemon slices. Serve hot or cold with white wine, crusty bread, and salad.

♦ *Serves 4*

Note: This sauce is great with any kind of grilled fish.

Grilled Sardines with Grape Leaves

SARDELES ME AMBELOFILLA

T he smoky flavor of this dish will make your mouth water. The grape leaves protect the delicate fish from breaking or sticking to the grill.

1 to 1½ pounds fresh sardines or
  any small fish
¼ cup olive oil, plus extra to
  brush grill
Juice of 2 lemons
3 cloves garlic, minced

½ teaspoon dried oregano
1 tablespoon chopped fresh thyme
Salt and freshly ground pepper
1 jar (16 ounces) grape leaves,
  rinsed and stems removed
Lemon wedges, for garnish

Clean sardines, leaving heads on, rinse with cold water, and drain in a colander. Place in a large bowl. In a medium bowl, combine oil, lemon juice, garlic, oregano, thyme, and salt and pepper; pour over fish and turn to coat. Cover and marinate in the refrigerator for 1 hour. Preheat grill and brush with oil. Remove fish from marinade and wrap 1 or 2 grape leaves around the center of each fish. Grill for 7 to 8 minutes on each side, or until cooked through. Remove from the grill, place on a platter, and serve hot with lemon wedges.

◆ *Serves 4 to 5*

Grilled Seafood Kabobs

Souvlaki me Thalasina

T ry this dish; it's scrumptious and healthy.

1 pound fresh swordfish, cut into
    1-inch cubes
¾ pound shrimp, shelled and
    deveined
½ pound sea scallops
1 medium onion, quartered and
    each layer separated

12 to 15 cherry tomatoes
2 red bell peppers, cut into
    small squares
Lemon wedges, for garnish

Marinade:

¼ cup olive oil, plus extra to oil grill
Juice of 1 to 2 lemons
3 cloves garlic, minced
1 tablespoon finely chopped fresh
    oregano

1 tablespoon fresh thyme
½ teaspoon paprika
Salt and pepper

In a large bowl, combine swordfish, shrimp, and scallops; set aside. In a medium bowl, combine olive oil, lemon juice, garlic, oregano, thyme, paprika, and salt and pepper and mix well. Pour marinade over the seafood and mix very gently to coat. Cover and refrigerate for 3 hours. Preheat and oil the grill. Remove seafood from marinade and reserve the liquid. Thread seafood pieces onto metal skewers, alternating it with onion, cherry tomatoes, and peppers. Grill seafood skewers, turning as needed, for 12 to 15 minutes, or until tender. Transfer skewers to a platter and garnish with lemon wedges. Serve hot with rice pilaf and salad.

◆ *Serves 4 to 5*

Grilled Swordfish Kabobs with Bay Leaves

Xifias Souvlaki

1½ to 2 pounds fresh swordfish, cut into 1-inch cubes	10 to 12 fresh bay leaves Lemon slices, for garnish

Marinade:

¼ cup olive oil, plus extra to oil grill Juice of 1 lemon ¼ cup white wine 2 tablespoons ouzo (optional)	3 cloves garlic, minced 2 tablespoons chopped fresh oregano 1 teaspoon paprika Salt and pepper

Wash and drain the swordfish. In a medium bowl, combine oil, lemon juice, wine, ouzo, garlic, oregano, paprika, and salt and pepper and mix well. Pour over fish and turn to coat. Cover and refrigerate for 3 hours. Preheat grill and brush with oil. Remove fish from marinade; reserve the liquid. Thread 5 or 6 swordfish cubes and some bay leaves on each kebob. Grill for 10 to 12 minutes, turning frequently and brushing with remaining marinade. Serve hot and garnish with lemon slices.

◆ *Serves 5 to 6*

Lemon Fried Red Mullet

BARBOUNIA TIGANITA ME LEMONI

S erve this dish with a tomato and cucumber salad, crusty bread, and your favorite wine.

1½ to 2 pounds whole fresh mullet	1 cup all-purpose flour
Juice of 1 lemon	Olive oil, for frying
Salt and pepper	Lemon slices, for garnish

Wash, clean, and drain the fish; sprinkle with the lemon and salt and pepper. Spread flour on a plate and flour each fish, shaking to remove excess. In large skillet, heat 1 inch olive oil until very hot. Fry fish until golden brown on both sides. Remove with a slotted spoon and drain on paper towels. Garnish with lemon slices. Serve hot.

◆ *Serves 4*

Lemon Grilled Lobster Tails

Psites Karavides

You must have ouzo with this delicious dish. Serve with salad and toasted crusty bread.

4 to 5 lobster tails

Juice of 2 lemons

3 tablespoons olive oil, plus extra
   to oil grill

3 cloves garlic, crushed

1 tablespoon chopped fresh oregano

1 teaspoon paprika

1 bay leaf, crushed

Salt and pepper

Oregano sprigs, for garnish

Lemon slices, for garnish

In a large bowl, combine lemon juice, oil, garlic, oregano, paprika, bay leaf, and salt and pepper. Add lobster tails and toss to coat, then cover and refrigerate for 3 hours. Preheat and oil the grill. Remove lobster tails from the marinade and cook for 10 to 12 minutes, turning frequently and brushing with remaining marinade. Remove from the grill and garnish with sprigs of oregano and lemon slices.

♦ *Serves 4 to 5*

Lobster on a plate.

Marinated Baked Mackerel

KOLIOS STO FOURNO MARINATA

1 ½ to 2 pounds fresh mackerel

Juice of 1 lemon

Salt and pepper

2 cups peeled and chopped fresh
ripe tomatoes, with juice

1 cup chopped onion

3 cloves garlic, minced

2 tablespoons chopped fresh flat
parsley

1 ½ tablespoons chopped fresh mint

½ cup white wine

¼ cup olive oil

Chopped parsley or mint,
for garnish

Clean, wash, and drain the fish and sprinkle with lemon juice and salt and
pepper. Cover and refrigerate for about 1 hour. Preheat the oven to 350 degrees. In a large bowl, combine tomatoes, onion, garlic, parsley, mint,
wine, olive oil, and salt and pepper and mix well. Place half of the tomato
mixture in a baking pan and cover with fish, then with remaining mixture.
Cook for 35 to 40 minutes, or until fish is fork tender. Remove from the
oven, pour sauce from the pan over fish, and sprinkle with chopped parsley
or mint. Serve hot with salad and crusty bread.

◆ *Serves 4 to 5*

Mykonos Grilled Shrimp Souvlaki

GARIDES PSITES SOUVLAKI

This dish is not only easy to make, it's scrumptious!

1 to 1½ pounds large shrimp, peeled, deveined, washed, and drained

Lemon slices, for garnish

Marinade:

¼ cup olive oil

Juice of 2 lemons

3 cloves garlic, minced

1 tablespoon honey

1 tablespoon chopped fresh oregano

2 bay leaves, crushed

½ teaspoon dried thyme

1 teaspoon dried sweet crushed red pepper

Salt and freshly ground pepper

Combine all marinade ingredients in a large bowl and mix well. Add shrimp and turn to coat well. Cover and refrigerate for 3 hours. Prepare the grill. Remove shrimp from marinade and thread 8 of them onto each skewer, being sure to pass the skewer through both the head and tail sections. Grill for 5 to 6 minutes on each side, or until shrimp turn pink. Garnish with lemon slices and serve with rice pilaf or salad.

◆ *Serves 4 to 5*

Shrimp Saganaki with Feta Cheese

GARIDES SAGANAKI

A delicious and easy dish, cooked in a skillet and topped with feta cheese.

1 to 1½ pounds shrimp, peeled, deveined, washed, and drained
Juice of 1 lemon
¼ cup olive oil
1 large onion, chopped
1 large green bell pepper, chopped
3 cloves garlic, chopped
1 cup peeled and chopped fresh tomatoes, with juice

¼ cup dry white wine
1 tablespoon chopped fresh flat parsley
½ teaspoon dried oregano
½ teaspoon dried basil
Salt and pepper
½ pound feta cheese, sliced

Sprinkle shrimp with the lemon juice and set aside. In a large skillet, heat oil and sauté onion, green pepper, and garlic, stirring, for 5 minutes. Add tomatoes, wine, parsley, oregano, basil, and salt and pepper and simmer over medium-low heat, stirring constantly, for 20 minutes. Add shrimp and stir until they turn pink. Top with feta slices and cook for 5 minutes, or until feta cheese has melted. Serve hot with bread to soak up all the delicious sauce.

◆ *Serves 4 to 5*

Shrimp with Ouzo

GARIDES ME OUZO

This delicious dish is one of the easiest dishes to make; it's also great as an appetizer or just as a light meal.

3 tablespoons olive oil

4 cloves garlic, thinly sliced

1 pound large fresh shrimp, peeled, deveined, washed, and drained

1 tablespoon chopped fresh oregano

1 bay leaf, crushed

Salt and pepper

3 tablespoons ouzo or brandy

Chopped fresh parsley, for garnish

In a large skillet, heat oil and sauté garlic for 1 minute; then add shrimp, oregano, bay leaf, and salt and pepper. Stir until the shrimp turn pink. Add ouzo or brandy, flame the shrimp, and cook for 2 or 3 more minutes. Spoon pan liquid over the shrimp and garnish with chopped parsley.

◆ *Serves 3 to 4*

Stuffed Squid with Rice

KALAMARAKIA GEMISTA

S erve this delicious dish with Greek salad, crusty bread, and a glass of retsina.

3 to 3½ pounds medium squid,
    cleaned and washed

¼ cup plus 2 tablespoons olive oil

1 large onion, finely chopped

3 cloves garlic, minced

1 cup uncooked long-grain
    white rice

1 tablespoon finely chopped
    fresh mint

2 tablespoons finely chopped
    fresh parsley

1½ cups peeled, seeded, and
    chopped fresh tomatoes

2 cups water

½ cup grated kefalotyri or
    Parmesan cheese

1 cup peeled and crushed fresh
    tomatoes

Salt and pepper

1 bay leaf

1 cinnamon stick

Preheat the oven to 350 degrees. Finely chop the squid's tentacles, leaving the bodies whole; drain in a colander. In a large, heavy skillet, heat ¼ cup of oil and sauté onion, garlic, and squid tentacles for 6 to 7 minutes. Add rice, mint, and parsley, stirring until rice is lightly browned, then add 1½ cups of the peeled, seeded, and chopped tomatoes and 1½ cups of the water, stirring 2 or 3 more times. Cover and simmer for 10 minutes, until liquid is almost completely absorbed and the rice is soft but only half-cooked. Remove from the heat and stir in cheese. Allow rice stuffing to cool enough to handle. With a teaspoon, carefully stuff squid bodies with the rice mixture, taking care not to overfill them. Use toothpicks to secure stuffing. Put squid in a baking pan, top with 1 cup of crushed tomatoes, 2 tablespoons of olive oil, and salt and pepper to taste. Add ½ cup of water, bay leaf, and cinnamon; cover with aluminum foil and bake for 1 hour, or until squid is tender. Add more water during cooking if necessary. Serve hot.

◆ *Serves 5 to 6*

FILLO DOUGH DIRECTIONS AND TIPS

I love working with fillo dough, and I create many of my delicious savory pies and pastries with this dough. Fillo is paper-thin and low in calories. I also like to use olive oil instead of butter on my fillo dough because it tastes better and is better for you.

1. If your fillo is frozen, thaw it in the refrigerator overnight.
2. To use fillo dough, unroll it onto a smooth, dry surface. Cover with plastic wrap and a damp towel keep covered until you're ready to use it.
3. Triangles: Take 2 fillo sheets and brush each with olive oil, covering the edges first and working toward the center. Place one on top of the other. Cut into 4 to 5 long strips and chill filling before using. Place 1½ to 2 teaspoons of filling in the middle bottom of each strip, then fold the right corner to the left to form a right triangle. Keep folding until you reach the end of the strip. Continue until you've used up all the filling and the fillo. Brush triangle tops with oil and sprinkle

lightly with water. This will maintain the shape of the fillo dough and keep it from cracking while it cooks. Bake according to recipe directions.

4. Roll up any remaining fillo, return it to the box, and refreeze.

5. When using fillo dough to make a whole pie, use 6 or 7 fillo sheets on the bottom and another 6 or 7 on the top and brush each one with olive oil: Place 6 or 7 sheets in a baking pan one on top of another, mound the filling in the center, and add 6 or 7 more sheets on top. Brush with olive oil and sprinkle lightly with water. Bake according to recipe directions.

Georgia on her television show, Cooking with Georgia.

Pasta and Rice Dishes

- Lasagna Pastitsio with Fillo Dough   204
- Lasagna with Chicken and Béchamel Sauce   206
- Lasagna with Leeks and Béchamel Sauce   208
- Pasta Topped with Artichokes and Feta   210
- Rice Pilaf with Vegetables   211
- Spaghetti with Ground Chicken Sauce   212
- Spaghetti with Meat Sauce   213
- Spaghetti with Tomato Sauce   214
- Stuffed Cannelloni with Meat   215
- Tomato Rice Pilaf   216

Lasagna Pastitsio with Fillo Dough

Pastitsio me Fillo

This is a classic dish served with salad.

1 package (16 ounces) ziti or penne pasta	1 ½ tablespoons chopped fresh mint
1 egg plus 2 egg whites	¼ cup white wine
1 cup grated kefalotyri or Parmesan cheese, divided	1 can (8 ounces) whole plum tomatoes, chopped, with juice
¼ cup olive oil	½ cup water
1 large onion, finely chopped	½ teaspoon ground cinnamon
3 cloves garlic, chopped	Pinch of nutmeg
2 tablespoons chopped fresh parsley	Salt and pepper
1 ½ to 2 pounds extra-lean ground beef	16 sheets fillo dough
	¼ cup olive oil, for brushing fillo

Preheat the oven to 350 degrees. Prepare pasta according to the package directions; rinse with cold water, drain, and set aside. Beat the egg and egg whites lightly, then add to the pasta, along with ½ cup of the cheese, and mix. In a medium saucepan, heat oil and sauté onion, garlic, and parsley, stirring, for 3 minutes, or until soft. Add ground beef and sauté until browned, stirring to break up the lumps. Slowly add the mint, wine, tomatoes, and ½ cup of water, then stir in cinnamon, nutmeg, and salt and pepper. Cover and simmer over medium heat for 25 minutes, or until most of the water has evaporated. Remove the pan from the stove, let stand for 10 minutes, then stir in the ½ cup of remaining cheese. Grease a 10 × 15 × 2½-inch baking pan and line 8 fillo sheets, brushing each with olive oil.

Spread half of the pasta mixture on top of the fillo, then top with the meat mixture and spread evenly. Arrange the remaining pasta on top of the meat in the same direction as before. Brush each of the remaining fillo sheets with oil and put them on top of the pasta. Trim any excess fillo and generously brush the top with oil. With a sharp knife, score the top into squares and sprinkle lightly with water. This will maintain the shape of the fillo dough and keep it from cracking. Bake for 50 minutes to 1 hour, or until golden brown on the top. Cool lightly before cutting and serve with salad.

◆ *Serves 6 to 8*

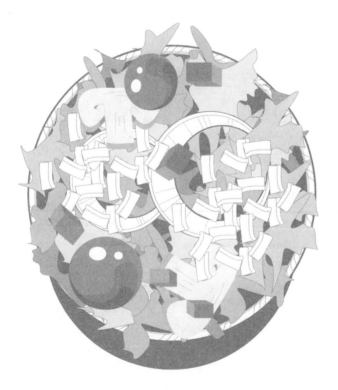

Lasagna with Chicken and Béchamel Sauce

PASTITSIO ME KOTA

1-pound package lasagna

Prepare lasagna according to package directions and drain.

3 eggs whites, beaten

1¼ cups grated kefalotyri or
   Parmesan cheese, divided

¼ cup olive oil

1 large onion, finely chopped

3 cloves garlic, minced

1½ to 2 pounds ground chicken
   breast

2 tablespoons chopped fresh basil

2 tablespoons chopped fresh
   parsley

½ cup white wine

1 cinnamon stick

2 whole cloves

2 cups peeled and chopped fresh
   tomatoes, with juice

½ cup water

Salt and pepper

2 tablespoons plain bread crumbs

Georgia-Style Béchamel Sauce
   (page 68)

Preheat the oven to 350 degrees. Put the cooked lasagna in a large bowl and add egg whites plus ½ cup of cheese. Mix together, being careful to not break the lasagna. In a medium saucepan, heat oil and add onion and garlic; sauté until tender, about 3 minutes. Add ground chicken and sauté, stirring constantly to break up lumps. Add basil, parsley, wine, cinnamon stick, cloves, tomatoes, ½ cup water, and salt and pepper. Stir to combine and simmer for 25 to 30 minutes, or until most of the water has evaporated. Remove the pan from the stove and let stand for 10 minutes, then add bread crumbs and ½ cup of cheese and mix well. Prepare the béchamel sauce. Grease a 9 × 15-inch baking pan; spread half of the lasagna mixture in the pan, then spread 1 cup of the béchamel sauce on top of the pasta. Spread the chicken mixture on top of that and arrange remaining lasagna on top of the chicken sauce. Top with remaining béchamel sauce and sprinkle with remaining ¼ cup of cheese. Bake for 50 minutes to 1 hour, or until the top is golden brown. Allow lasagna to cool for 25 to 30 minutes before cutting. I know you'll love this dish with béchamel sauce.

◆ *Serves 6*

Variation: You may substitute ground turkey for the ground chicken.

Lasagna with Leeks and Béchamel Sauce

PASTITSIO ME PRASA

L eeks make this vegetarian pasta dish delectable.

2 large bunches leeks (about 3
    pounds), roots cut off and any
    yellow leaves removed
¼ cup olive oil
3 cloves garlic, minced
2 tablespoons chopped fresh flat
    parsley
Salt and pepper

1 package (16 ounces) pastitsio
    (or penne) pasta
2 egg whites (save yolks to
    prepare béchamel sauce)
½ cup grated kefalotyri or
    Parmesan cheese
2 to 3 large tomatoes, thinly sliced
¾ cup crumbled feta cheese

Preheat the oven to 350 degrees. Rinse leeks thoroughly, then drain and slice the white parts and about 1 inch of green leaves. In a large skillet, heat the oil and sauté leeks, garlic, parsley, and salt and pepper to taste, stirring, for 10 minutes. Remove from the heat and cool. Prepare pasta according to the package directions, then rinse with cold water and drain. Lightly beat the egg whites and pour over the pasta; add the Parmesan cheese and mix well.

Béchamel sauce:

4 tablespoons (½ stick) butter

5 tablespoons flour

3 cups hot milk

2 egg yolks

¼ cup grated kefalotyri or
Parmesan cheese

Pinch of nutmeg

½ teaspoon salt

In a medium saucepan, melt the butter, stir in the flour, and continue stirring for 1 to 2 minutes. Add hot milk and keep stirring to attain a smooth and creamy consistency. Remove saucepan from the heat. Beat egg yolks lightly, add the cheese; stir in 1 cup of the hot mixture and beat well. Return egg mixture to saucepan and add nutmeg and salt, stirring consistently over low heat until mixture is thick and smooth. Grease a 10 × 15 × 2½-inch baking pan. Arrange half of the pasta in the pan, spread leek mixture over the pasta, layer the tomato slices, sprinkle with crumbled feta cheese, and top with the remaining pasta. Pour the béchamel sauce over the pasta and spread evenly. Bake for 50 minutes or until lightly golden brown on top. Let stand at least 20 minutes before serving.

◆ *Serves 6 to 8*

Pasta Topped with Artichokes and Feta

AGINARES ME MACARONIA

This is my mother's favorite dish to prepare in the spring with fresh artichokes from the garden. It takes only 30 to 40 minutes to prepare, so it's great for any time. Serve with bread and a glass of white wine.

¼ cup olive oil

1 cup chopped onions

4 cloves garlic, crushed

½ cup chopped red bell pepper

2 cups peeled and chopped fresh
    tomatoes

1 tablespoon tomato paste

1 cup water

1 teaspoon chopped fresh
    oregano

2 (10-ounce) packages frozen
    artichoke hearts, or

    2 (14-ounce) cans artichoke
    hearts, quartered

Salt and pepper

1 teaspoon chopped fresh parsley

½ cup sliced kalamata olives

1 pound linguine

¾ cup feta cheese diced into
    small pieces

In a large skillet, heat oil and sauté onion, garlic, and red pepper for 5 minutes. Add tomatoes, tomato paste, oregano, and 1 cup water. Cover and simmer over medium heat for 20 minutes, or until sauce thickens. Stir in artichoke hearts, salt and pepper, parsley, and olives and cook for 10 minutes, adding more water if necessary. Meanwhile, prepare pasta according to package directions and drain. Arrange cooked pasta on a large platter and cover with this delicious sauce. Sprinkle with diced feta cheese and serve hot.

◆ *Serves 6*

Rice Pilaf with Vegetables

Rizi me Hortarika

¼ cup olive oil

1 large onion, finely chopped

½ cup chopped celery

½ cup chopped carrots

3 cloves garlic, chopped

2 cups uncooked long-grain
   white rice

4 cups chicken broth

Salt and pepper

1 cup fresh or frozen peas

1 tablespoon chopped fresh parsley

Heat the oil in a medium saucepan and sauté the onion, celery, carrots, and garlic for 5 minutes. Add the rice and stir for 2 minutes; then add chicken broth and salt and pepper to taste. Stir the mixture 2 or 3 times, cover, bring to a boil, and cook for 10 minutes. Stir in peas and parsley. Lower the heat and cook until the liquid is absorbed, about 15 minutes, or until rice is tender. Remove from the heat and let stand for 5 minutes. Serve as a side dish.

◆ *Serves 5 to 6*

Spaghetti with Ground Chicken Sauce

MACARONIA ME KIMA KOTAS

This is a very healthful, quick, and easy dish to make.

¼ cup olive oil

1 large onion, finely chopped

3 cloves garlic, finely chopped

1½ pounds ground chicken or
   turkey breast

2 tablespoons chopped
   fresh mint

3 to 4 tomatoes, peeled, seeded,
   and chopped, with juice

½ teaspoon ground cinnamon

Salt and pepper

1 cup water

1 pound spaghetti

¾ cup grated Parmesan cheese

Heat the oil in a medium saucepan and sauté the onion and garlic for 5 minutes, then add ground chicken, stirring until cooked through, about 7 minutes. Add mint, tomatoes, cinnamon, salt and pepper, and 1 cup of water. Cover, reduce heat to medium, and simmer for about 40 minutes, or until most of the liquid is absorbed. Meanwhile, bring a large pot of water to a boil and cook the pasta according to package directions. Drain the pasta, arrange on a warm platter, add chicken sauce, and sprinkle with cheese. Serve hot with salad and bread. This dish is traditionally made with ground beef or lamb, but I like it better with chicken.

♦ *Serves 5 to 6*

Spaghetti with Meat Sauce

MACARONIA ME KIMA

Spaghetti with meat sauce is my son George's favorite dish; he can have it every day and not get sick of it. It's a quick and easy dish to make.

¼ cup olive oil

1 large onion, finely chopped

3 cloves garlic, chopped

1 cup sliced fresh mushrooms

2 pounds lean ground beef

1 tablespoon finely chopped
   fresh mint

1 tablespoon finely chopped fresh
   flat parsley

¼ cup white wine

1½ cups fresh peeled and crushed
   tomatoes or canned crushed
   tomatoes

1 stick cinnamon

Salt and pepper

1 cup water

1 pound spaghetti

½ cup grated kefalotyri or
   Parmesan cheese

Heat the oil in a saucepan and sauté onion and garlic for about 3 minutes. Add mushrooms and sauté, stirring, for 3 more minutes. Add ground beef and stir until well browned. Stir in mint, parsley, wine, tomatoes, cinnamon, salt and pepper to taste, and 1 cup of water. Reduce heat to medium and simmer for about 35 to 40 minutes, stirring often, until most of the liquid is absorbed. Meanwhile, cook the pasta according to package directions. Remove cinnamon stick from the sauce. Drain pasta and arrange on a large platter; sprinkle with some of the cheese, then cover with the meat sauce. Sprinkle additional cheese on top and serve hot with garlic bread and salad.

◆ *Serves 6*

Spaghetti with Tomato Sauce

MACARONIA ME TOMATA

This is a wonderful thick sauce to use as the basis for other recipes.

¼ cup olive oil

1 large onion, finely chopped

3 cloves garlic, finely chopped

1 can (28 ounces) whole peeled
  tomatoes, chopped, with juice

1 tablespoon tomato paste

1 tablespoon chopped fresh mint

¼ teaspoon dried oregano

Salt and pepper

½ cup water

1 pound spaghetti or other pasta

½ cup grated kefalotyri or
  Parmesan cheese

Chopped fresh mint, for garnish

In a large saucepan, heat the oil and sauté onion and garlic for 5 minutes. Add tomatoes, tomato paste, mint, oregano, salt and pepper, and ½ cup of water. Cover and allow the sauce to simmer for about 30 minutes, stirring occasionally with a wooden spoon. Meanwhile, cook pasta according to package directions and drain. Arrange pasta on a warm platter, cover with sauce, and sprinkle with the cheese. Garnish with chopped mint and serve hot with salad.

◆ *Serves 4 to 5*

Stuffed Cannelloni with Meat

KANELLONIA YEMISTA

1 pound cannelloni or manicotti
   shells

¼ cup olive oil

½ cup finely chopped onion

2 cloves garlic, finely chopped

1½ pounds extra-lean ground beef

¼ cup white wine

1 cup crushed tomatoes, with juice

½ teaspoon ground cinnamon

½ teaspoon dried mint

Salt and pepper

1¼ cups water, divided

1 cup grated kefalotyri or
    Parmesan cheese, divided

1½ cups canned crushed tomatoes

1 tablespoon olive oil

Preheat the oven to 350 degrees. Cook cannelloni shells according to package directions, rinse with cool water, and drain well, taking care not to break them. In a large skillet, heat oil and sauté onion and garlic for 5 minutes. Add ground meat and stir with a wooden spoon until well browned. Stir in wine, 1 cup of tomatoes with juice, cinnamon, mint, salt and pepper, and ½ cup of the water. Cover and simmer for 25 to 30 minutes, or until most of the liquid is absorbed. Remove from the heat and cool for 10 minutes. Add ½ cup of the grated cheese to the meat mixture and stir well. Using a teaspoon, fill shells with the meat mixture. Place the stuffed shells in a greased 10 × 13 × 2½-inch baking pan. Cover with 1½ cups canned crushed tomatoes, drizzle with olive oil, season with salt and pepper to taste, and add about ¾ cup of water. Sprinkle with the remaining ½ cup of cheese, cover with aluminum foil, and bake for 35 minutes, or until sauce is thickened, adding more water if necessary during cooking. Let stand for 10 minutes before serving with salad and crusty bread.

♦ *Serves 5 to 6*

Tomato Rice Pilaf

PILAFI ME TOMATA

This is my sister Grigoria's favorite rice pilaf; my mother makes it a lot in the summer with fresh garden tomatoes.

3 tablespoons olive oil

1 large onion, finely chopped

4 cloves garlic, finely chopped

2 cups uncooked long-grain white rice

1½ cups peeled and chopped fresh tomatoes, with juice

1 tablespoon finely chopped fresh basil

2 tablespoons finely chopped fresh mint

3½ cups chicken broth

Salt and pepper

In a large saucepan, heat oil and sauté onion and garlic for 5 minutes, or until soft. Add rice and cook, stirring, for 2 minutes, or until golden. Add tomatoes, basil, and mint and stir, then add chicken broth and salt and pepper to taste. Cover, bring to boil, and cook for 10 minutes. Reduce heat to low and cook for 20 more minutes, or until liquid is absorbed. Remove from the heat and let stand for 5 minutes. Serve hot as a side dish with chicken or any roast.

◆ *Serves 6*

GREEK SPIRITS

Ouzo

Ouzo, the tradition and soul of Greece, is a clear and a strongly flavored liqueur. Served with ice cubes and a little water and great with meze (appetizers), ouzo is the star of the table when you're with a group of friends in a restaurant or tavern.

Brandy

Greece produces an assortment of brandies; it's a common drink for Greeks on a night out on the town. The most popular brandies in Greece are:

Achaia Clauss: Liqueur brandy aged seven years or longer, from Achaia

Anglias (Haggipavlu): Delicate brandy from Cyprus

Cambas: One of the best brandies, aged 10 years or longer, from Attica and the Peloponnese

Metaxas: Full-bodied brandy aged five to seven years, from Piraeus

Sans Rival: Delicate brandy aged five years, from Piraeus

Mastiha

Mastiha, a clear gum mastiha-flavored liqueur, is extremely popular in Greece. It comes from Chios Island, home to more than four million mastiha trees. With it unique sweet flavor, mastiha is also used in Greek cooking. It is sold in a small jar and looks like crystals.

Greek Wines

The most enjoyable drink on the Greek table is wine. We all know the delight a good wine can add to a meal. Even the best-cooked dish becomes bland when it is consumed without a fine glass of wine. Greek wines seem to be made for Greek appetizers, such as fried keftethes (fried meatballs), spiced feta cheese, fried cheese saganaki, and garlic feta cheese spread.

The most popular wines in Greece are:

White wines:
Kouras Patras (Kourtaki): Dry, medium-bodied, aromatic white, limey, mineral flavor, from Patras
Kretikos (Boutari): Dry, medium-bodied, a good soft fruit palate, mineral flavor, from Crete
Mantinia (Calligas): Dry, full-bodied white, medium acidity, a spicy peach fruit, from Cephalonia
Santorini (Boutari): Crisp, well-balanced dry white, balance of berry, citrus, hazelnut, and mineral flavors, from Santorini

Red Wines:
Chateau Carras (Carras): A full-bodied dry red made with a blend of Cabernet and Merlot, medium tannin, high acidity, a berry flavor, from Limnos

Monte Nero (Calligas): A full-bodied dry red, heavy tannin, medium acidity, a smoky berry, mineral flavor, from Cephalonia

Naoussa (Boutari, Tzantalis): Strong red wine that spends at least one year in oak

Nemea (Boutari, Kourtaki, Cambas): Dry, robust wine packed with fruit, a berry flavor

Ruby (Calligas): A light, easy-drinking, dry red, from Cephalonia

Dessert Wines:

Muscat: Rich, sweet wines with a scent of Muscat on the palate, great with dessert

Mavrodaphne (Partraiki, Achaia Clauss, Cambas): Sweet, rich red wine, also served on the rocks as an aperitif or in a punch

Grand Commandaria (Haggipavlu): Sweet, rich red wine, a great vintage-port-style wine

Georgia and her daughter, Daisy.

Pizzas and Calzones

- Calzone Stuffed with Meat   222
- Calzone with Spinach and Feta Filling   224
- Daisy's Chicken Calzone   225
- Garlic and Basil Pizza   226
- Peter's Greek-Style Pizza   227
- Pizza with Artichokes and Feta   229
- Pizza with Meatballs   230
- Pizza with Olives and Artichokes   232
- Pizza with Spinach and Feta   233
- Shrimp Pizza   234

Calzone Stuffed with Meat

KALTSOUNIA GEMISTA ME KIMA

This calzone is delicious for lunch or dinner. For a complete meal all you need is a delicious Greek salad and a glass of good wine.

1 recipe basic pizza dough

3 tablespoons olive oil

1 large onion, chopped

1 large carrot, chopped

1 cup sliced mushrooms

3 cloves garlic, chopped

1 pound extra-lean ground beef

1 can (28 ounces) plum tomatoes, chopped, with juice

2 tablespoons chopped parsley

½ teaspoon dried basil

Salt and pepper

¾ cup diced kaseri or fontina cheese

¼ cup grated kefalotyri or Parmesan cheese

2 tablespoons plain bread crumbs

Preheat the oven to 400 degrees. In a large skillet, heat the oil and add onion, carrots, mushrooms, and garlic. Cook, stirring, for 6 to 7 minutes. Add ground beef and sauté, stirring constantly, until the meat begins to brown. Add the tomatoes, parsley, basil, and salt and pepper. Lower the heat, cover, and simmer until the liquid has been absorbed, about 15 to 20 minutes. Remove from the heat and let cool for 20 to 25 minutes. Stir in all of the cheese and the bread crumbs and mix well. Divide the dough into 4 or 5 equal portions. On a lightly floured surface, roll each one into a ½-inch-thick circle. Spread 2½ to 3 tablespoons of filling onto one half of each circle, then fold in half and press the edges tightly to seal. Cut slits on the top to allow steam to escape. Bake for 30 minutes, or until crust is golden brown. Serve hot or warm.

♦ *Serves 4 to 5*

Pizza dough:

1 envelope active dry yeast	1½ teaspoons salt
1¾ cups warm water, divided	3 tablespoons olive oil, plus extra
1 teaspoon sugar	to oil the bowl
3½ cups bread flour	2 teaspoons white vinegar

In a medium bowl, mix the yeast with 1 cup of the warm water, sugar, and ½ cup of bread flour. Let mixture stand for 10 to 15 minutes to proof the yeast. In a large bowl, sift the remaining flour with the salt. Make a well in the center of the flour and add the yeast mixture, remaining ¾ cup of warm water, olive oil, and vinegar. Stir with a wooden spoon until a dough forms. Sprinkle with more bread flour as needed. Remove the dough from the bowl and place on a floured surface. Knead for 8 to 10 minutes until the dough is smooth, elastic, and no longer sticky. Brush a large bowl with olive oil, place the dough in the bowl, and sprinkle the top with bread flour. Cover with plastic wrap and let rise 50 minutes to an hour. Punch the dough down, remove it from the bowl, place it on a lightly floured surface, and roll out into a circle. Place the circle on a 10-inch pizza pan and press the edges to make a thin rim. Cover and let rest for 25 to 30 minutes, then finish with your choice of toppings.

◆ *Serves 4 to 6*

Note: You can also divide the dough into 2 balls and make 2 10-inch thin-crust pizzas.

Calzone with Spinach and Feta Filling

KALTSOUNIA ME SPANAKI KAI FETA

This calzone is delicious and very easy to prepare.

1 recipe basic pizza dough
   (see page 223)
2 cups washed, dried, and finely
   chopped fresh spinach leaves
1 cup crumbled feta cheese
½ cup grated kefalotyri or
   Parmesan cheese

1 egg, beaten
2 cloves garlic, minced
1 tablespoon chopped fresh dill
¼ cup finely chopped green onions
Salt and ground pepper

Preheat the oven to 400 degrees. In a large bowl, combine spinach, feta, kefalotyri, beaten egg, garlic, dill, green onion, and salt and pepper. Mix well with a wooden spoon and set aside. Divide the dough into 4 or 5 equal portions. On a lightly floured surface, roll each one into a ½-inch-thick circle. Spread 2½ to 3 tablespoons of filling onto one half of each circle, then fold in half and press the edges tightly to seal. Cut slits on top of dough to allow steam to escape. Bake for 30 minutes, or until crust is golden brown. Serve hot or warm.

◆ *Serves 4 to 5*

Daisy's Chicken Calzone

KALTSOUNIA GEMISTA ME KOTA

1 recipe basic pizza dough
    (see page 223)
2 cups cooked and diced chicken
    breast
¾ cup cubed feta cheese
1 can (14 ounces) artichoke hearts,
    drained and diced
¼ cup pitted and chopped
    kalamata olives

2 tablespoons chopped fresh dill
1 tablespoon chopped fresh parsley
2 cloves garlic, chopped
1 bunch green onions, chopped
1 egg, beaten
3 tablespoons grated kefalotyri or
    Parmesan cheese
Salt and pepper

Preheat the oven to 400 degrees. In a large bowl, combine chicken, feta, artichokes, olives, dill, parsley, garlic, onion, beaten egg, kefalotyri cheese, and salt and pepper to taste. Divide the dough into 4 or 5 equal portions. On a lightly floured surface, roll each one into a ½-inch-thick circle. Spread 2½ to 3 tablespoons of filling onto one half of each circle, then fold in half and press the edges tightly to seal. Cut slits on the top to allow steam to escape. Bake for 30 minutes, or until crust is golden brown. Serve hot with a salad.

◆ *Serves 4 to 5*

Garlic and Basil Pizza

Pizza me Basiliko kai Skordo

1 recipe basic pizza dough
   (see page 223)
1 can (28 ounces) plum tomatoes,
   drained well and diced
4 cloves garlic, thinly sliced
2 tablespoons chopped fresh
   sweet basil

½ teaspoon dried oregano
1 tablespoon olive oil
Salt and pepper
½ pound kaseri or mozzarella
   cheese, diced
½ cup diced feta cheese
1 tablespoon olive oil

Preheat the oven to 400 degrees. In a medium bowl, combine tomatoes, garlic, basil, oregano, olive oil, and salt and pepper. Mix well and set aside. On a lightly floured surface, roll out the dough into a circle and place in an oiled pizza pan. Push the edges up to make a thin rim about ¼ inch high. Cover and let stand for 30 minutes. Spread the tomato mixture evenly on top of the pizza dough, then spread the feta and mozzarella or kaseri and drizzle with olive oil. Bake for 20 to 25 minutes, or until the crust is golden brown.

◆ *Serves 4 to 5*

Peter's Greek-Style Pizza

PETER'S PIZZA

This is my husband, Peter's, recipe; he's the best pizza maker!

1 recipe basic pizza dough
   (see page 223)
Olive oil, for brushing the pizza
2 tablespoons grated kefalotyri or
   Parmesan cheese

1 cup diced mozzarella cheese
1 cup diced kaseri or
   fontina cheese

Tomato sauce:

3 tablespoons olive oil
1 medium onion, finely chopped
2 cloves garlic, crushed
1 can (28 ounces) plum tomatoes,
   chopped, with juice
1 tablespoon tomato paste

1 tablespoon finely chopped
   fresh oregano
½ teaspoon dried mint
½ teaspoon dried basil
½ teaspoon sugar
Salt and pepper

Preheat the oven to 400 degrees. In a medium saucepan, heat the oil and sauté the onion and garlic for 5 minutes, or until softened. Add the tomatoes, tomato paste, oregano, mint, basil, sugar, and salt and pepper to taste; mix well. Cover, bring to a boil, and simmer over low heat for 25 minutes, stirring occasionally with a wooden spoon, until the sauce is quite thick. Remove from the heat and let cool. Oil a pizza pan and stretch the dough with your hands to make it fit. Put it in the pizza pan and push up the edges

to make a thin rim about ¼ inch high. Cover and let rise for 25 to 30 minutes. Brush the crust with olive oil, sprinkle the kefalotyri or Parmesan
cheese, spread tomato sauce evenly over the pizza, and top with mozzarella
and kaseri cheese. Bake for 18 to 20 minutes, or until the edges are golden
brown. Serve hot.

♦ *Serves 3 to 4*

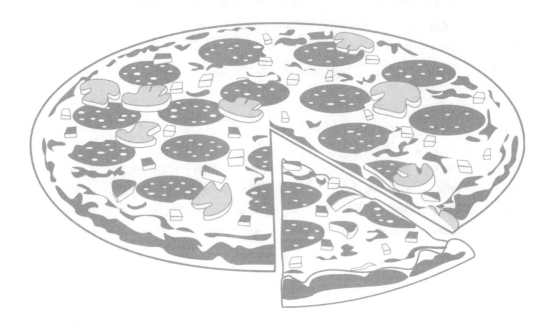

Pizza with Artichokes and Feta

PIZZA ME AGINARES KAI FETA

The artichokes and feta cheese make this pizza delicious and unique.

1 recipe basic pizza dough
  (see page 223)
3 to 4 plum tomatoes, peeled,
  seeded, and chopped
2 tablespoons finely chopped
  fresh basil
3 cloves garlic, chopped
½ teaspoon grated kefalotyri or
  Parmesan cheese

2 tablespoons dried oregano
Salt and pepper
2 (14-ounce) cans artichoke hearts,
  drained and diced
½ pound feta cheese, diced
1 tablespoon olive oil

Preheat the oven to 400 degrees. Lightly brush a pizza pan with oil. On a lightly floured surface, roll out the dough into a circle, then place it in the pizza pan; push up the edges to make a thin rim about ¼ inch high. Cover and let rise for 25 to 30 minutes. In a medium bowl, combine tomatoes, basil, garlic, cheese, oregano, and salt and pepper to taste; mix well. Spread the tomato mixture evenly over the pizza, arrange the artichoke hearts on top, and sprinkle with the diced feta. Drizzle with a little olive oil and bake for 15 to 20 minutes, or until edges are golden brown. Serve hot.

♦ *Serves 3 to 4*

Pizza with Meatballs

Pizza me Keftethakia

This is another delicious pizza, served with salad.

1 recipe basic pizza dough
  (see page 223)

Tomato sauce:

3 tablespoons olive oil

3 cloves garlic, crushed

1½ cups canned crushed tomatoes

1 tablespoon tomato paste

¼ cup dry white wine

½ teaspoon dried oregano

½ teaspoon dried mint

½ teaspoon dried basil

½ teaspoon sugar

Salt and pepper

Preheat the oven to 400 degrees. In a medium saucepan, heat the oil and sauté the garlic for a minute. Add crushed tomatoes, tomato paste, wine, oregano, mint, basil, sugar, and salt and pepper to taste. Cover and bring to a boil, then simmer over a low heat for 15 to 20 minutes, stirring occasionally with a wooden spoon until the sauce is quite thick. Remove from the heat and set aside to cool.

Meatball mixture:

1 pound extra-lean ground beef
   or lamb

1 small onion, grated

2 cloves garlic, crushed

1 tablespoon finely chopped fresh
   flat parsley

1 tablespoon finely chopped
   fresh mint

3 tablespoons plain bread crumbs

1 egg white, lightly beaten

Salt and pepper

¼ cup olive oil

1 large onion, thinly sliced

½ pound kaseri or mozzarella
   cheese, diced

3 tablespoons grated kefalotyri or
   Parmesan cheese

In a large bowl, combine the meat, small onion, garlic, parsley, mint, bread crumbs, lightly beaten egg white, and salt and pepper to taste; mix well. Divide the mixture into small balls (about 15) and refrigerate for 25 to 30 minutes. In a large skillet, heat the oil, then add the meatballs and fry them until browned on all sides. Remove meatballs from the skillet and drain on paper towel. Oil the pizza pan and stretch the dough with your hands. Then place it in the pizza pan and push up the edges to make a thin rim, about ¼ inch high. Cover and let rise for 25 to 30 minutes. Spread tomato sauce evenly over the pizza dough and close to the edge. Top with onion slices, then arrange the meatballs on the pizza and sprinkle with kaseri cheese and grated cheese. Bake for 18 to 20 minutes, or until the edges are golden brown.

◆ *Serves 4*

Variation: You can also make the meatballs with ground turkey or chicken.

Pizza with Olives and Artichokes

PIZZA ME ELIES KAI AGINARES

I love this pizza; it's so easy to make.

1 recipe basic pizza dough
   (see page 223)
2 cups peeled, drained, and diced
   fresh plum tomatoes
1 medium onion, chopped
3 cloves garlic, finely chopped
2 tablespoons chopped fresh mint
½ teaspoon dried oregano

1 can (14 ounces) artichoke hearts,
   drained and diced
1 tablespoon olive oil
¾ cup pitted and coarsely chopped
   kalamata olives
Salt and pepper
½ pound kaseri or mozzarella
   cheese, diced

Preheat the oven to 400 degrees. Lightly brush a pizza pan with oil. On a lightly floured surface, roll out the dough into a circle, place it in a pizza pan, and push up the edges to make a thin rim about ¼ inch high. Cover and let rise for 30 minutes. In a large bowl, combine the tomatoes, onion, garlic, mint, oregano, artichoke hearts, olive oil, olives, and salt and pepper; mix well. Spread the tomato mixture evenly over the pizza dough and close to the edge. Spread the cheese on top and bake for 20 to 25 minutes, or until the edges are golden brown.

◆ *Serves 4 to 5*

Pizza with Spinach and Feta

Pizza me Spanaki kai Feta

Try this delicious pizza with spinach and feta cheese, one of my daughter Daisy's favorites.

1 recipe basic pizza dough
  (see page 223)
¼ cup plus 1 tablespoon olive oil
1 medium onion, chopped
1 pound fresh spinach, washed,
  drained, and chopped

2 tablespoons chopped fresh dill
3 cloves garlic, chopped
Salt and pepper
1 cup diced feta cheese
¼ pound kaseri or fontina cheese,
  diced

Preheat the oven to 400 degrees. Brush pizza pan with oil. On a lightly floured surface, roll out the dough into a circle and place in the pizza pan. Push up the edges to make a thin rim about ¼ inch high. Cover and let stand for 25 to 30 minutes. In a large skillet, heat ¼ cup oil and sauté onion for 3 minutes, or until soft and translucent. Add the spinach, dill, garlic, and salt and pepper and cook, stirring, until wilted. Remove from the heat and drain the liquid. Spread half the feta onto the pizza dough, spread the spinach evenly on top of the feta, and then spread the remaining feta on top, along with the kaseri. Drizzle about 1 tablespoon olive oil on top of the pizza and bake for 20 minutes, or until edges are golden brown. Serve hot.

♦ *Serves 4*

Shrimp Pizza

Pizza me Garides

This is a delightful pizza served with salad and wine.

1 recipe basic pizza dough (see page 223)	Salt and pepper
3 tablespoons olive oil	1½ cups diced kaseri or mozzarella cheese
3 cloves garlic, thinly sliced	1 tablespoon olive oil
1 pound medium shrimp, shells and tails removed	

Tomato sauce:

4 plum tomatoes, peeled, seeded, and diced	1 tablespoon finely chopped fresh oregano
2 tablespoons finely chopped fresh mint	1 tablespoon olive oil
	Salt and pepper

Preheat the oven to 400 degrees. In a large skillet, heat the oil and cook the garlic and shrimp, stirring, until shrimp turn pink. Add salt and pepper to taste. Remove from the skillet, drain the liquid, and set aside. In a medium bowl, combine tomatoes, mint, oregano, oil, and salt and pepper; mix well. Oil the pizza pan and stretch the dough. Place it in the pan and push up the edges to make a thin rim, about ¼ inch. Cover and let rise for 25 to 30 minutes. Spread the tomato mixture evenly over the pizza, arrange the shrimp over the tomato mixture, sprinkle cheese on top, and drizzle with a little olive oil. Bake for 15 to 20 minutes, or until the edges are golden brown. Serve hot.

◆ *Serves 4*

Pies and Tarts

- Pastry Tips   236
- Artichoke Feta Cheese Tart   237
- Cabbage Sausage Fillo Rolls   239
- Cheese Pie   241
- Chicken Rice Fillo Rolls   242
- Classic Lamb Rolls with Fillo Dough   244
- Meat Pie with Pine Nuts   246
- Spinach and Feta Cheese Tart   248
- Spinach Pie   249
- Tart with Shrimp and Feta Cheese   251
- Village Chicken Pie   253

PASTRY TIPS

1. Some Greek pastries call for a syrup topping. There are two ways to add syrup to a cake.

   a. For a hot cake that just came out of the oven, you would add cold syrup.
   b. For a cold cake that has had time to cool after coming out of the oven, you would add hot syrup.

   Adding lemon juice to hot syrup prevents it from thickening.

2. When preparing any pastry, make sure you have all of the ingredients premeasured and ready in front of you.
3. Flour tip: When a recipe calls for 3 to 4 or 5 to 6 cups of flour, use your own judgment to get the right consistency.

Artichoke Feta Cheese Tart

Tarta me Aginares

A rtichoke feta cheese tart is my daughter Daisy's favorite. You're going to love it as much as she does.

1 recipe 9-ounce pastry tart dough
    (see page 251)

Filling:

¼ cup olive oil	Salt and pepper
1 large onion, thinly sliced	1 cup crumbled feta cheese
½ cup chopped scallions	½ cup grated kefalotyri or
2 (14-ounce) cans artichoke hearts,	Parmesan cheese, plus extra for
drained and halved	topping
2 tablespoons chopped fresh dill	¼ cup milk
1 tablespoon chopped fresh parsley	2 large eggs, lightly beaten

Preheat the oven to 350 degrees. Heat the oil in a large skillet and sauté the onion, stirring, for 6 to 7 minutes. Add scallions, artichoke hearts, dill, parsley, and salt and pepper and cook for 5 to 6 more minutes. Remove from the heat and cool for 15 minutes. Place the mixture in a large bowl. In a medium bowl, combine feta, grated kefalotyri or Parmesan, lightly beaten

Artichoke feta cheese tart.

eggs, and milk; mix well. Combine cheese mixture with artichoke mixture and stir, then pour into tart dough already in the tart pan. Sprinkle with cheese and bake for 50 minutes to 1 hour, or until golden brown. Remove from the oven and let cool for 20 minutes before serving.

◆ *Serves 6*

Cabbage Sausage Fillo Rolls

LAXANOPITA ME LOUKANIKO ROLLO

Try these delicious cabbage rolls; they are great for lunch or dinner.

1 pound Greek loukaniko or sweet
  Italian sausage

¼ cup olive oil

1 large onion, chopped

3 cloves garlic, finely chopped

1 medium red bell pepper, chopped

1 to 1½ pounds green cabbage,
  blanched, drained, and thinly
  sliced

2 tablespoons chopped fresh
  parsley

1 tablespoon dried mint

Salt and pepper

2 eggs, plus 1 egg white

1 cup grated Parmesan cheese

1 pound fillo dough

¼ cup olive oil, for brushing fillo

Chopped parsley, for garnish

Preheat the oven to 350 degrees. In a large skillet, lightly brown the sausage on all sides. Remove, drain on paper towel, and dice. In a large saucepan, heat oil and sauté onion, garlic, and red pepper for 5 minutes. Add the sliced cabbage, parsley, mint, and salt and pepper and cook, stirring, for 15 minutes, or until cabbage is tender. Remove from the heat and cool for 10 minutes. Place cabbage in a large bowl and add the sausages. In a medium bowl, beat eggs and egg whites and the grated Parmesan cheese. Add this mixture to the cabbage and toss well. Using 2 fillo sheets for each roll, brush each sheet with oil, and stack them. Put 3 tablespoons of the cabbage mixture in the middle of one short edge of the fillo. Fold the end over, then fold in both sides, and roll up into a neat package. Repeat until you've used all of the mixture. Brush a cookie sheet with oil and place rolls on it about 1 inch apart. Brush top of the rolls with olive oil and sprinkle some water on top to prevent the fillo from cracking. Bake for 35 to 40 minutes or until golden brown. Let stand for 5 minutes and arrange onto a platter garnished with parsley. Serve with salad.

◆ *Serves 6*

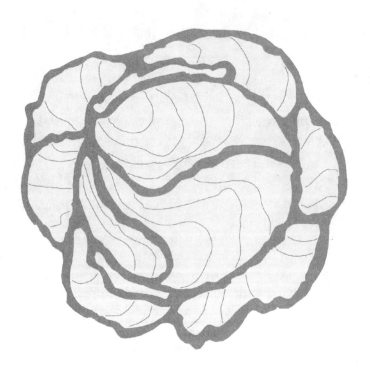

Cheese Pie

Tyropita

For me, anytime is a good time for a piece of my tyropita. I just love it, and it's so easy to prepare.

1 pound feta cheese, crumbled

½ cup grated kefalotyri cheese or Parmesan cheese

½ cup farmer's cheese

¼ cup milk

⅛ teaspoon nutmeg

1 tablespoon finely chopped fresh flat parsley

2 large eggs, beaten

White pepper, to taste

1 pound fillo dough

¼ cup olive oil, for brushing fillo

Preheat the oven to 350 degrees. In a large bowl, combine, feta, kefalotyri, farmers cheese, milk, nutmeg, parsley, beaten eggs, and white pepper to taste; mix well with a fork. Grease the bottom of a 10-inch circle pan with oil. Line the pan with 7 fillo dough sheets, brushing each sheet with oil. Spread the cheese mixture evenly in the pan and fold any overhanging fillo into the pan. Brush each of the remaining fillo sheets with oil and place on top of the cheese mixture. Trim any excess fillo dough and brush the top with oil. With a sharp knife, score the top into squares, but do not cut all the way through. Sprinkle with water and bake for 35 to 40 minutes, or until top is golden brown. Serve hot or warm.

◆ *Serves 10 to 12*

Chicken Rice Fillo Rolls

RIZOKOTOPITA ME FILLO

This healthful pie can be served at lunch or dinner with a salad.

1½ to 2 pounds chicken breast

¼ cup olive oil, plus extra for
    brushing fillo

1 large onion, finely chopped

1 large red bell pepper, chopped

½ cup chopped carrots

3 cloves garlic, crushed

¾ cup uncooked long-grain
    white rice

2 tablespoons chopped fresh
    flat parsley

½ teaspoon dried mint

Salt and pepper

1½ cups chicken broth

1 egg, beaten, plus 1 egg white

¾ cup crumbled feta cheese

¼ cup grated kefalotyri or
    Parmesan cheese

1 pound fillo dough

Preheat the oven to 350 degrees. Wash the chicken, pat dry, and cut into very small pieces. Heat ¼ cup olive oil in a large skillet and sauté onion, red pepper, carrots, and garlic for 5 minutes. Add chicken and sauté for another 7 to 8 minutes, then add rice, parsley, mint, and salt and pepper and stir. Add the broth, lower the heat, and cook, stirring frequently, for 10 to 15 minutes, or until the liquid has been absorbed and the rice softened. Remove the skillet from heat and cool slightly. Put the mixture in a large bowl. In a small bowl, lightly beat the eggs and all cheese; add to the chicken mixture and combine well. Take 2 sheets of the fillo dough, brush each thoroughly with oil, and stack them. Then place 3 tablespoons of the chicken mixture in the middle of one short edge of the fillo. Fold the end over, fold both sides in, then roll up into a neat package. Repeat until all of the filling has been used. Brush a baking pan with oil and place rolls on it about 1 inch apart. Brush olive oil on the top of each roll and sprinkle with a little water to prevent the fillo from cracking. Bake for 35 to 40 minutes, or until top is golden brown. Serve hot.

♦ *Serves 6 to 8*

Classic Lamb Rolls with Fillo Dough

Arni Bourekia me Fillo

These delicious lamb rolls are a great treat, especially for dinner or any occasion!

2½ to 3 pounds leg of lamb

¼ cup olive oil, plus extra for
    brushing fillo

1 large onion, finely chopped

3 cloves garlic, chopped

1 large red bell pepper, chopped

½ cup chopped celery

1 tablespoon chopped fresh mint
    or ½ teaspoon dried mint

2 tablespoons chopped fresh parsley

½ cup white wine

1½ cups peeled and chopped fresh
    tomatoes

½ teaspoon dried oregano

1 cinnamon stick

2 whole cloves

¾ cup water

Salt and pepper

1 egg, lightly beaten

1 cup diced kefalotyri cheese
    (or any hard yellow cheese)

2 tablespoon plain bread crumbs

1 pound fillo dough

Preheat the oven to 350 degrees. Wash the lamb, pat dry, and cut into very small pieces. In a large saucepan, heat the olive oil and sauté lamb until lightly brown. Add onion, garlic, red pepper, celery, mint, and parsley and cook, stirring, for 7 minutes. Add the wine, stir 1 to 2 more times, then add tomatoes, oregano, cinnamon, cloves, water, and salt and pepper. Cover and simmer for 50 minutes to 1 hour, adding a little water if necessary. Cook, stirring occasionally, until meat is tender and liquid has been absorbed. Remove from the heat, cool slightly, and move to a large bowl. Add lightly beaten egg, cheese, and bread crumbs; mix well. Brush 2 sheets of fillo with oil and stack them. Place take 3 tablespoons of the meat mixture in the middle of one short edge of the fillo. Fold that end over, fold both sides in, and roll up into a neat package. Repeat until all of the filling has been used. Place rolls on to a baking pan, about 1 inch apart, brush with oil, and sprinkle with water to prevent the fillo from cracking. Bake for 50 minutes or until golden brown. Serve hot on a platter with rice pilaf and salad or cut into pieces and serve as an appetizer.

◆ *Serves 6 to 8*

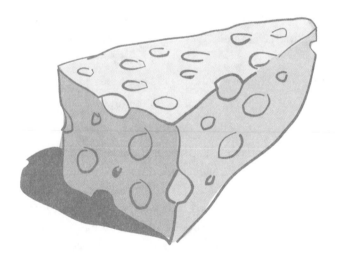

Meat Pie with Pine Nuts

KREATOPITA

These meat pies are delicious with salad.

¼ cup olive oil, plus extra for
    brushing fillo
1 large onion, finely chopped
1 medium red bell pepper, chopped
3 cloves garlic, crushed
2½ pounds extra-lean ground beef
2 tablespoons finely chopped
    fresh mint
1 tablespoon finely chopped fresh
    parsley

¼ cup white wine
3 large tomatoes, peeled and
    chopped, with juice
Salt and pepper
¼ cup pine nuts
½ cup grated kefalotyri or
    Parmesan cheese
3 tablespoons plain bread crumbs
2 eggs, beaten
1 pound fillo dough

Preheat the oven to 350 degrees. In a large saucepan, heat the oil and sauté the onion, red pepper, and garlic, stirring, for 5 minutes. Add the ground beef and cook, stirring constantly, until it browns. Stir in mint, parsley, and wine, then add the tomatoes, salt and pepper to taste, and pine nuts. Lower the heat and simmer until all of the liquid has been absorbed, 15 to 20 minutes. Remove from the heat and let stand for 15 to 20 minutes to cool. When the meat mixture has cooled, stir in the cheese, bread crumbs, and beaten eggs; mix well. Lightly oil the bottom of a 12-inch round baking pan and line it with 7 sheets of fillo dough, brushing each sheet with oil as you add it to the pan. Spread the meat mixture evenly over the fillo, fold over any overhanging fillo leaves, and brush them with oil. Add remaining sheets of fillo on top, brushing each layer with oil. Trim any excess fillo dough and brush the top with oil, sprinkle with water, and score with a sharp knife. Bake the pie for about 45 minutes or until golden brown on top. Cool for 20 minutes before serving.

◆ *Serves 6 to 8*

Spinach and Feta Cheese Tart

TARTA ME SPANAKI KAI FETA

1 recipe 9-ounce pastry tart dough
   (see page 251)

Filling:

¼ cup olive oil

1 large onion, finely chopped

½ cup chopped fresh fennel,
   with leaves

¼ cup finely chopped dill

½ cup chopped scallions

1 package (10 ounces) fresh spinach,
   wash, drained, and chopped

Salt and pepper

¾ cup crumbled feta cheese

¼ cup milk

2 eggs

¼ cup grated kefalotyri or
   Parmesan cheese, plus extra
   for topping

Preheat the oven to 350 degrees. In a large skillet, heat the oil and sauté onion, fennel, dill, and scallions for 5 minutes, or until soft. Add the spinach and cook, stirring, for 10 minutes. Add salt and pepper, remove from the stove and cool slightly, then place the spinach mixture into a bowl. In a medium bowl, combine feta cheese, milk, eggs, and kefalotyri, stirring well with a fork. Combine cheese mixture and spinach mixture; mix well. Pour mixture into tart dough already in the tart pan and sprinkle with cheese. Bake for 50 minutes to 1 hour, or until golden brown. Cool for 20 minutes before cutting into pieces.

♦ *Serves 6*

Spinach Pie

Spanakopita

This pie is a favorite in every Greek household! Once you get the hang of making it, you'll want to have it often because it's so delicious.

¼ cup olive oil, plus extra for
    brushing fillo
1 large onion, finely chopped
2 bunches scallions, chopped
1 bunch fresh dill, chopped
1 bunch fresh parsley, chopped
1 bunch fresh fennel with leaves,
    chopped
2 to 2½ pounds fresh spinach,
    washed, drained, and chopped
    into small pieces

2 large eggs
½ pound feta cheese, crumbled
½ cup grated kefalotyri or
    Parmesan cheese
Salt and pepper
1 pound fillo dough

Preheat the oven to 350 degrees. Heat olive oil in a medium saucepan and sauté the onion, scallions, dill, parsley, and fennel for 6 to 7 minutes. Add the spinach and stir for 10 minutes, or until it is wilted. Remove from the heat and drain all the liquid through a colander. Transfer to a large bowl and set aside to cool. In a medium bowl, beat the eggs and stir in the feta. Add to the spinach mixture, sprinkle with kefalotyri cheese and salt and pepper to taste, and mix. Oil the bottom of a medium-size (9 × 13 × 2½ inches) baking pan and line with 7 fillo dough sheets, brushing each fillo sheet with oil. Spread the spinach mixture evenly in the pan, folding any overhanging fillo into the pan. Brush each of the remaining fillo sheets with oil and place on top of the spinach mixture. Trim any excess fillo dough and brush the top with more oil. With a sharp knife, score the top into squares, but do not cut all the way through. Sprinkle with water and bake for 35 to 40 minutes, or until golden brown. Served hot or cold with salad, this can be a meal in itself.

♦ *Serves 6 to 8*

Tart with Shrimp and Feta Cheese

TARTA ME GARIDES

This delicious tart can be enjoyed at room temperature with a salad.

Pastry crust:

1½ to 2 cups all-purpose flour

½ teaspoon baking powder

1 teaspoon salt

½ cup olive oil or ½ cup cold
   butter, cut into pieces

1 egg, beaten

¼ cup or more cold water

1 teaspoon white vinegar

2 tablespoons grated Parmesan
   cheese

Preheat the oven to 350 degrees. To make the pastry crust, sift the flour, baking powder, and salt into a large bowl. Add the olive oil or butter and rub with your fingertips. Stir in beaten egg, water, vinegar, and Parmesan cheese; knead on a lightly floured surface until smooth. Roll out the pastry crust and use it to line a 9-inch tart pan. Chill for 30 minutes.

Shrimp filling:

1 pound medium shrimp

3 tablespoons olive oil

1 large onion, thinly sliced

1 red bell pepper, chopped

1 cup sliced mushrooms

1 tablespoon chopped fresh
   flat parsley

1 tablespoon chopped fresh mint
   or 1 teaspoon dried mint

2 cloves garlic, minced

¼ cup dry wine

2 medium tomatoes, peeled and
   chopped

Salt and pepper

¾ cup crumbled feta cheese

1 large tomato, sliced

2 tablespoons grated kefalotyri or
   Parmesan cheese

Peel and devein the shrimp, remove the tails, rinse with water, pat dry, and dice. In a large skillet, heat the oil and sauté the onion and red pepper for 5 minutes. Add mushrooms, parsley, mint, and garlic and stir for 2 to 3 minutes. Add the shrimp, wine, tomatoes, and salt and pepper and cook, stirring, for 7 to 8 minutes. Remove from the heat and drain any liquid. Place mixture into large bowl and cool slightly. Add the feta and stir together. Spread the mixture evenly in the tart pan, top with tomato slices and sprinkle with Parmesan cheese. Bake for 50 minutes to 1 hour, or until golden brown. Serve at room temperature.

◆ *Serves 6*

Village Chicken Pie

XORIATIKI PITA

This pie can be served as a main course.

¼ cup olive oil, plus extra for
   brushing fillo

1 large onion, finely chopped

3 cloves garlic, minced

½ cup chopped celery

2 medium potatoes, peeled
   and cubed

1½ pounds chicken breast, cubed

1 cup sliced mushrooms

1 medium red bell pepper, chopped

2 tablespoons chopped fresh parsley

1 teaspoon dried oregano

½ teaspoon dried mint

Salt and pepper

1 cup chicken broth

1 cup cubed feta cheese

½ cup grated kefalotyri or
   Parmesan cheese, plus extra
   for topping

1 egg

½ cup milk

Pinch of nutmeg

12 fillo sheets

Preheat the oven to 350 degrees. In a large skillet, heat oil and sauté onion, garlic, and celery for 5 minutes. Then add the potatoes, chicken, mushrooms, and red pepper and sauté for 6 to 7 minutes more. Stir in parsley, oregano, mint, salt and pepper, and chicken broth. Reduce heat to low and simmer for 20 minutes, or until all of the liquid evaporates. Remove from heat and cool for 15 minutes. Move the mixture to a large bowl. In a medium bowl, mix feta, kefalotyri, egg, milk, and nutmeg, stirring with a fork; then add to the chicken mixture. Mix all of the ingredients well. Brush a 9 × 13 × 1½-inch baking pan with oil and line with 6 sheets of fillo dough, brushing each sheet with oil. Spread the mixture evenly in the pan and fold any overhanging fillo into the pan. Brush each of the remaining fillo sheets with oil and place on top. Trim any excess fillo dough, brush the top with oil, and score the top into squares, being careful not to cut all the way through. Sprinkle with water and bake for 35 to 40 minutes, or until golden brown. Let cool 20 minutes, cut into pieces, and serve with salad.

◆ *Serves 6*

Desserts

- Butter Cookies with Hazelnuts   256
- Cookie Twists   257
- Copenhagen Walnut and Fillo Dough Pastry   258
- Georgia's Cheesecake Baklava   260
- Georgia's Chocolate Cream Cheese Cake   262
- Georgia's Famous Baklava with Olive Oil   264
- Honey Fritters   266
- Kataifi Shredded Fillo Pastry with Walnuts and Pistachio Nuts   268
- Orange Cake   270
- Revani Cake with Yogurt   271
- Secret Kiss Kourambiethes Cookies   273
- Semolina Pudding with Raisins and Pine Nuts   275
- Stuffed Melomakarona Honey-Dunked Cookies   277
- Sweet Cream Cheese Fillo Triangles   279
- Sweet Easter Bread   280
- Traditional Lucky New Year's Sweet Bread   282

Butter Cookies with Hazelnuts

KOURAMBIETHES ME FOUNDOUKIA

This recipe comes from my sister Despina's kitchen. Kourambiethes are the traditional butter cookies for the holidays in Greece. I remember my sister making these cookies all the time because she had a sweet tooth; she would eat the whole tray herself!

1 pound (4 sticks) sweet butter, room temperature	3½ to 4 cups all-purpose flour
1 cup confectioners' sugar	1 teaspoon baking powder
2 egg yolks	1½ cups roasted, skinned, and chopped hazelnuts or almonds
¼ cup ouzo or cognac	3 cups confectioners' sugar, for topping
1 teaspoon vanilla	
1 teaspoon lemon zest	

Preheat the oven to 350 degrees. Beat the butter and sugar until light and fluffy. Add the egg yolks one at a time, beating well after each addition. Add ouzo, vanilla, and lemon zest. Sift flour and baking powder, then slowly add the flour mixture and hazelnuts to the batter until it is stiff enough to be able to pinch off a piece and form a ball. Cover and let dough stand for 30 minutes at room temperature. Shape individual tablespoons of dough into half-moon or round cookie shapes. Place on a greased cookie sheet 1 inch apart. Bake for 20 to 25 minutes, or until light golden brown. Cool in the pan for 5 minutes, then set the warm cookies ½ inch apart on aluminum foil and sift confectioners' sugar over them to coat heavily. Store at room temperature for up to 2 weeks.

♦ *Yields 3 dozen*

Cookie Twists

KOULOURAKIA

These delicious cookies, a traditional Easter treat, are also perfect for dunking in coffee or tea.

1 cup (2 sticks) unsalted butter
½ cup vegetable oil
1½ cups sugar
4 large eggs
¼ cup fresh-squeezed orange juice
1 tablespoon anise-flavored
   liqueur extract

1 teaspoon vanilla
4½ to 5 cups bread flour
   (approximately)
4 teaspoons baking powder
1 to 2 egg yolks, for glaze

Preheat the oven to 350 degrees. In a large bowl, combine butter, oil, and sugar and beat until creamy and smooth. Add the eggs, orange juice, anise flavoring, and vanilla and beat for 5 minutes. Sift together flour and baking powder and add gradually to the batter until a soft dough forms. Let stand for 20 minutes. Pinch off a piece of dough equal to about 1 to 1½ tablespoons and roll into a 5-inch rope. Fold the rope in half and twist together. Arrange twisted ropes on a greased cookie sheet 1 inch apart and brush with egg wash. Bake for 20 to 25 minutes, or until golden brown. Cool on wire racks and store in a cookie jar.

◆ *Yields 3½ to 4 dozen*

Copenhagen Walnut and Fillo Dough Pastry

KOPENHAG

This is a classic dessert and very easy to make.

¾ cup sugar

4 large eggs, yolks and whites separated

½ cup (1 stick) unsalted butter, softened

3 tablespoons cognac or rum

1 teaspoon vanilla

1 cup dry bread crumbs

1 teaspoon baking powder

1 teaspoon ground cinnamon

½ teaspoon ground cloves

2 cups chopped walnuts

12 fillo sheets

Melted butter, for brushing fillo

Preheat the oven to 350 degrees. In a large bowl, beat the sugar and 4 egg yolks until creamy; add butter and continue beating. Add cognac or rum and vanilla. In a separate bowl, beat 4 egg whites until they form stiff peaks. Combine the bread crumbs, baking powder, cinnamon, clove, and walnuts; set aside. Fold together the egg whites and the bread crumb mixture alternately with the egg yolk and sugar batter until thoroughly blended. Grease a 10 × 13 × 2½-inch baking pan. Layer 6 sheets of fillo dough in the pan, brushing each layer with butter. Pour batter mixture over the fillo, fold in the sides of the fillo, and brush with butter. Top with the 6 remaining fillo sheets, brushing each one with butter and trimming off any excess. Brush the top leaf with butter and, with sharp knife, mark the top into diamond shapes. Sprinkle with a little water and bake for 45 to 50 minutes, or until the fillo turns golden. Remove from the oven, let stand 5 minutes, then spoon the cold syrup (see below) on top. Cool in the pan for 5 to 6 hours before serving.

Syrup:

2 cups sugar	¼ cup fresh-squeezed orange juice
2½ cups water	1 cinnamon stick

In a medium saucepan, bring all ingredients to a boil, then cook for 6 to 7 minutes over medium heat. Remove the pan from the heat and set aside to cool.

◆ *Serves 10 to 12*

Georgia's Cheesecake Baklava

BAKLAVA KEIK ME TYRI

I f you think baklava is delicious, try this cheesecake baklava with its unique flavor that keeps you coming back for more. This treat is great for special occasions.

Crust:

2 cups graham cracker crumbs

½ cup finely chopped walnuts

½ teaspoon ground cinnamon

4 tablespoons (½ stick) unsalted butter, melted

Cheese filling:

3 (8-ounce) packages cream cheese, softened

1 cup sugar

½ cup sour cream

2 tablespoons all-purpose flour

3 large eggs

2 teaspoons vanilla extract

1 tablespoon freshly squeezed lemon juice

Baklava filling:

1½ cups chopped walnuts

2 tablespoons graham cracker crumbs

1 teaspoon ground cinnamon

⅛ teaspoon ground cloves

2 tablespoons sugar

2 tablespoons unsalted butter, melted, plus extra for brushing fillo

15 sheets fillo dough

Preheat the oven to 325 degrees. In a large bowl, combine graham cracker crumbs, walnuts, cinnamon, and butter and mix well. Brush a 9-inch spring-form pan with butter, then press the mixture on the bottom of the pan and ½ inch up the side. Set aside.

To make the cheese filling, beat cream cheese in large bowl of electric mixer; add sugar, sour cream, and flour, beating continuously. Add the eggs, one at a time, vanilla, and lemon juice and beat until smooth. Pour mixture into prepared springform pan.

To make the baklava filling, combine walnuts, graham cracker crumbs, cinnamon, clove, sugar, and butter in a medium bowl; mix well. Stack 15 fillo sheets and cut them into 9-inch rounds. Brush each round piece with melted butter and set 5 of them on top of the cheesecake filling. Sprinkle fillo with half of the walnut mixture and top with 5 more fillo rounds, brushing each with butter. Sprinkle with remaining walnuts and top with remaining 5 sheets of fillo, brushing each one with butter. With a sharp knife, score the top in wedges; do not cut through the entire pastry. Brush the top with butter and sprinkle with a few drops of water, to hold the shape of the fillo and keep it from cracking. Bake for 1½ hours or until golden brown. Remove from the oven and let stand for 5 minutes, then spoon the cool syrup (see below) on top. Cool, then refrigerate for 8 to 10 hours before serving.

Syrup:

1 cup sugar
1½ cups water
1 strip lemon peel

2 whole cloves
1 teaspoon freshly squeezed lemon
   juice, strained

In a small saucepan, combine sugar, water, lemon peel strip, cloves, and lemon juice, stirring, bring to a boil, and cook for 8 to 10 minutes.

◆ *Serves 8 to 10*

Georgia's Chocolate Cream Cheese Cake

Tourta me Tyri

This cheesecake is as attractive as it is delicious.

Chocolate crumb crust:

1½ cups vanilla graham cracker
    crumbs
2 tablespoons sugar
2 tablespoons cocoa
    powder

4 tablespoons (½ stick) unsalted
    butter, melted, plus extra for
    buttering pan
¼ cup finely chopped almonds
1 teaspoon vanilla

Cheese filling:

3 (8-ounce) packages cream
    cheese, softened
¼ cup cocoa powder
½ cup sour cream
1 teaspoon vanilla
2 teaspoons ouzo or brandy
3 tablespoons flour

3 eggs
1 cup drained and chopped
    maraschino cherries
Whipped cream, for garnish
Chocolate curls, for garnish
Whole maraschino cherries,
    for garnish

Preheat the oven to 350 degrees. To make the crust, in a large bowl, combine graham cracker crumbs, sugar, cocoa powder, melted butter, almonds, and vanilla and mix well. Butter a 9-inch springform pan and press the mixture to the bottom of the pan and ½ inch up the side. Bake for 10 minutes, remove from the oven, and cool. Turn the oven up to 400 degrees.

To make the filling, combine cream cheese, cocoa powder, sour cream, vanilla, and ouzo in large bowl of electric mixer and beat until smooth. Add flour and the eggs, one at time, and beat well. Stir in the chopped cherries, then pour batter into prepared crumb crust. Bake for 10 minutes, without opening the oven door, then reduce the temperature to 250 degrees and continue baking for another 35 to 40 minutes. At the end of that time, the cake may not appear to be set in the middle. Turn off the oven and leave the cheesecake in it for 30 minutes without opening the door. Remove from the oven, using a knife loosen the cake from the sides, and cool to room temperature. Remove the sides of the pan and refrigerate overnight. Before serving, garnish with whipped cream, chocolate curls, and whole cherries.

◆ *Serves 8 to 10*

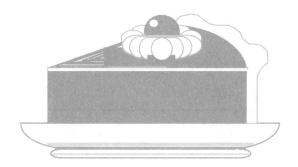

Georgia's Famous Baklava with Olive Oil

BAKLAVA

This is the most popular pastry in Greece. My mother makes her baklava with olive oil instead of butter. It tastes much better and it's better for you. Try it!

5 cups coarsely chopped walnuts

½ cup sugar

¼ cup plain dried bread crumbs

1 tablespoon ground cinnamon

1 teaspoon ground cloves

¾ cup olive oil, divided

1 teaspoon vanilla

1 pound fillo dough

Preheat the oven to 325 degrees. In a large bowl, mix the walnuts, sugar, bread crumbs, cinnamon, and cloves. Add ¼ cup of the olive oil and the vanilla and mix well. Brush olive oil on the sides and bottom of an 18 × 12 × 3-inch jelly roll pan. Layer 5 sheets of fillo in the pan, brushing each layer with olive oil. Spread 1½ cups of the walnut mixture evenly over the top layer of fillo, then fold in the long sides of the fillo and brush them with oil. Add 3 more fillo sheets, brushing each with olive oil, and spread with 1½ cups of the walnut mixture. Turn the long sides of the fillo toward the center and brush with oil. Add 3 more fillo sheets, brushing each one with olive oil, and top with remaining walnut mixture. Turn the sides in and continue adding the remaining fillo sheets, brushing each with oil. With a sharp knife, cut diagonally across the top to mark diamond-shaped pieces, but do not cut all the way through. Brush with oil until all sides and the top are completely covered. Sprinkle with water and bake for 1 hour or until golden brown.

Syrup:

2 cups sugar

3 cups water

½ cup honey

1 stick cinnamon

3 whole cloves

2 tablespoons freshly squeezed
lemon juice

1 strip lemon peel

Mix together all of the syrup ingredients and boil for 8 to 10 minutes. Remove the cinnamon, cloves, and lemon peel strip and cool completely. Spoon the cold syrup over the hot baklava and let the baklava stand at room temperature for 6 hours before serving. Do not refrigerate.

◆ *Yields 3 dozen*

Honey Fritters

LOUKOUMATHES

Serve with honey syrup.

Dough:

1 envelope active dry yeast	½ teaspoon salt
2 cups warm water	1 teaspoon sugar
3½ cups bread flour	Olive oil, for frying

Syrup:

1 cup water	¾ cup honey
1 cup sugar	1 cinnamon stick

Vegetable oil for frying	Ground cinnamon
½ cup finely chopped walnuts	

Prepare the syrup before frying the loukoumathes. Combine the water, sugar, honey, and cinnamon and boil slowly for 8 to 10 minutes, until the syrup is thick. In a large bowl, dissolve the yeast in 1 cup of warm water, then stir in 1 cup of bread flour. Cover bowl with a heavy towel and allow it to rise for 20 minutes. Then stir in the salt, sugar, and remaining water and bread flour and allow it to rise for 1 hour, or until doubled in bulk (this should be a thick batter, not a dough). In a deep frying pan, heat 5 to 6 inches of oil until very hot (365 degrees). Drop dough by tablespoonfuls into the hot oil (dough will slide off the spoon easily if you dip the spoon in water before you take each spoonful) and fry the balls until they puff up and rise to the surface of the oil, or until they turn golden brown. Remove from the oil and drain on paper towels. Arrange the loukoumathes on a platter, slowly pour the syrup over them, and sprinkle lightly with walnuts and cinnamon. Serve hot or warm.

◆ *Yields 2½ to 3 dozen*

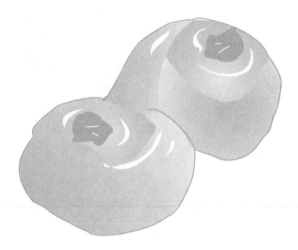

Kataifi Shredded Fillo Pastry with Walnuts and Pistachio Nuts

KATAIFI

This dessert is very popular in Greece. The filling is similar to baklava except that it is made with shredded fillo and rolled.

Filling:

2 cups coarsely chopped walnuts	½ teaspoon ground cloves
1 cup chopped pistachio nuts	¼ cup sugar
3 tablespoons dried bread crumbs	2 teaspoons vanilla
1 teaspoon ground cinnamon	2 tablespoons spiced rum or ouzo

1 package kataifi dough (available in any Greek market)	¾ cup (1½ sticks) unsalted butter, melted, divided

Preheat the oven to 350 degrees. In a large bowl, mix the walnuts, pistachios, bread crumbs, cinnamon, cloves, sugar, vanilla, and rum and set aside. Unwrap kataifi dough on a clean flat surface. Pull it apart and cut in lengths 5 to 6 inches long. Put 1 tablespoon of the walnut mixture at the end of a piece and roll up to form a log about 3 inches long. Start rolling tightly and gradually loosen as you reach the end. Continue until you use up all of the filling and the kataifi dough. Arrange rolls 1 inch apart on a greased cookie sheet, brush with melted butter, and bake for 30 to 35 minutes, or until golden brown. Remove from the oven, spoon the warm syrup (see below) on top, cover with a towel, and let rest for 6 to 8 hours before serving.

Syrup:

2 cups sugar

3 cups water

¼ cup honey

2 whole cloves

1 tablespoon freshly squeezed
    lemon juice

In a medium saucepan, combine of all the syrup ingredients, bring to a boil, and cook for 12 to 15 minutes. Remove the cloves before using.

◆ *Yields 1½ dozen*

Orange Cake

KEIK ME PORTOKALI

Y ou'll love this cake with a cup of coffee or tea.

3 cups all-purpose flour

3 teaspoons baking powder

½ teaspoon salt

1 cup (2 sticks) unsalted butter,
   room temperature

1½ cups sugar

4 eggs

1 tablespoon orange zest

1 teaspoon lemon zest

½ cup fresh-squeezed orange juice

1 teaspoon vanilla

½ cup roasted and chopped
   almonds

Confectioners' sugar, for topping

Preheat the oven to 350 degrees. In a large bowl, sift together the flour, baking powder, and salt; set aside. Beat butter and sugar until creamy, then add eggs one at a time, beating continuously. Add orange zest, lemon zest, orange juice, and vanilla, then slowly add the flour and almonds and beat on low speed until blended. Grease a 9-inch Bundt or tube pan with butter. Pour batter into the pan and bake for 1 hour, or until a wooden toothpick inserted in the center comes out clean. Cool in the pan for 10 minutes, then remove and cool on a rack. Sprinkle with confectioners' sugar.

♦ *Serves 8 to 10*

Revani Cake with Yogurt

REVANI

Revani cake is a very popular Greek dessert and my son Peter's favorite.

2 cups flour

1½ cups farina semolina

1 tablespoon baking powder

1 cup (2 sticks) unsalted butter,
   room temperature

1 cup sugar

6 large eggs, separated

1 tablespoon lemon zest

2 teaspoons vanilla

1½ cups plain yogurt

1 cup blanched, roasted, and
   coarsely chopped almonds

Preheat the oven to 350 degrees. In a large bowl, combine flour, farina semolina, and baking powder and set aside. In a large bowl, beat butter and sugar until creamy, then add egg yolks, lemon zest, vanilla, and yogurt; beat together. In a separate bowl, beat the egg whites until they are stiff. Alternately fold the egg whites and the flour mixture into the butter mixture, making sure they are well blended. Pour batter into a greased 9 × 13 × 2½-inch pan or a 10 × 2-inch round pan and bake for 45 minutes to 1 hour, or until golden brown.

Syrup:

2 cups sugar

2½ cups water

1 teaspoon freshly squeezed
    lemon juice

1 strip lemon peel

In a medium saucepan, boil all of the syrup ingredients for 8 to 10 minutes. When the cake is cool, cut it into diamond-shaped pieces and slowly spoon hot syrup all over the top. Let stand for 3 to 4 hours at room temperature, then serve.

◆ *Serves 10 to 12*

Secret Kiss Kourambiethes Cookies

KOURAMBIETHES GEMISTI ME SOKOLATA

These are the most delicious cookies. You have to try them!

1 cup blanched almonds

1 pound prewhipped unsalted
   butter

2 egg yolks

1 cup confectioners' sugar

3 tablespoons ouzo or brandy

2 teaspoons lemon zest

1 teaspoon vanilla

3 to 3½ cups all-purpose flour
   (approximately)

1 teaspoon baking powder

1 bag (6 ounces) Hershey milk
   chocolate Kisses

3 cups confectioners' sugar,
   for topping

Preheat the oven to 350 degrees. Lightly roast the almonds in an un-
greased skillet over low heat until they are a very light golden brown;
chop and set aside. In the large bowl of an electric mixer, beat the butter,
egg yolks, sugar, ouzo, lemon zest, and vanilla. Beat for 10 minutes until
smooth and creamy. Sift together the flour and baking powder, then
slowly add 2 cups of the flour and the almonds to the batter and knead by
hand. Add remaining flour in ¼-cup increments until just enough flour
has been added to make the dough silky and smooth. Let dough rest for
30 minutes at room temperature. Remove wrappers from the Kisses,
shape 1 tablespoon of dough around each chocolate, then roll to make a
ball. Be sure to cover each chocolate piece completely. Arrange on an un-
greased cookie sheet about 1 inch apart and bake for 15 to 20 minutes, or
until cookies are a pale yellow color. Remove cookie sheet from the oven

and cool in pan for 5 minutes, then place cookies on aluminum foil and sift confectioners' sugar on them until they are completely covered. Let stand 15 to 20 minutes. Place each cookie in a paper baking cup and store at room temperature for up to 2 weeks.

◆ *Yields 2½ to 3 dozen*

Semolina Pudding with Raisins and Pine Nuts

HALVAS

This traditional Greek pudding is a great treat anytime.

Syrup:

2½ cups sugar

4 cups water

1 teaspoon grated lemon peel

1 teaspoon freshly squeezed
lemon juice

1 cinnamon stick

Pudding:

½ cup (1 stick) unsalted butter

½ cup olive oil

2 cups semolina (pasta flour)

½ cup golden raisins

¾ cup pine nuts, toasted

¼ cup toasted and chopped pine
nuts, for garnish

1 tablespoon ground cinnamon,
plus extra for garnish

In a large pan, combine all of the syrup ingredients, bring to a boil, and cook for 10 minutes. Remove cinnamon stick and cool slightly. In a large saucepan, heat the butter and oil until very hot, then slowly add the semolina and keep stirring with a wooden spoon over medium–low heat until the semolina is lightly browned. Add the raisins, ¾ cup pine nuts, and cinnamon; then slowly add the syrup to the semolina mixture and stir constantly over low heat for 10 minutes, until the syrup is absorbed and the mixture is thickened. Remove from the heat, pour the pudding into a 10 × 13 × 2½-inch pan and cool until set. Unmold onto a platter, garnish with chopped pine nuts, and sprinkle with cinnamon.

◆ *Serves 8 to 10*

Stuffed Melomakarona Honey-Dunked Cookies

Melomakarona Gemista

These cookies are traditionally made for Christmas but I love making them all the time.

4½ to 5 cups all-purpose flour

1 teaspoon baking powder

½ teaspoon baking soda

½ teaspoon salt

2 teaspoons ground cinnamon

1 teaspoon ground cloves

1½ cups light olive oil

¾ cups sugar

Juice of 1 large orange

1 tablespoon orange zest

¼ cup cognac

Ground walnuts, for sprinkling

Stuffing:

1 cup chopped walnuts

2 tablespoons honey

1 teaspoon vanilla

½ teaspoon cinnamon

Preheat the oven to 350 degrees. In a large bowl, sift together flour, baking powder, baking soda, salt, cinnamon, and cloves and set aside. Beat the oil and sugar for 10 minutes or until creamy. Add the orange juice, orange zest, and cognac and beat together for 5 or 6 more minutes. Add the flour mixture to the liquid gradually, stirring with a wooden spoon after each addition, until a dough forms. Knead, adding a little more flour if necessary, until the dough is soft but not stiff.

To make the stuffing, combine the walnuts, honey, vanilla, and cinnamon in a medium bowl and stir all together. Shape 1½ to 2 tablespoon of dough into a cylinder and stuff with 1 teaspoon of the walnut mixture and shape. Continue with the remaining dough and stuffing. Arrange cylinders on a greased cookie sheet about 1 inch apart and bake for 25 to 30 minutes, or until golden brown. Remove from the oven and cool on a wire rack. Dip the cooled cookies into the hot syrup (see below), soak for a few minutes, drain, arrange on a platter, and sprinkle with ground walnuts. Serve at room temperature. Delicious for any time.

Syrup:

1 cup sugar

1 cup honey

1½ cups water

1 cinnamon stick

1 strip orange zest

In a medium saucepan, bring all the syrup ingredients to a boil and cook over medium heat for 8 to 10 minutes.

◆ *Yields 2½ to 3 dozen*

Sweet Cream Cheese Fillo Triangles

TIROPITAKIA GLYKA ME TYRI

Sweet cream cheese fillo dough triangles are a delicious treat. Serve them at room temperature.

2 (8-ounce) packages cream
   cheese, room temperature

1 cup sugar

3 tablespoons honey

2 eggs yolks

1 tablespoon lemon zest

1 teaspoon vanilla

1 pound fillo dough

4 tablespoons (½ stick) unsalted
   butter, melted

Confectioners' sugar, for topping

Ground cinnamon, for dusting

Preheat the oven to 350 degrees. Combine cream cheese, sugar, and honey and beat with an electric mixture on medium speed for about 3 minutes. Add egg yolks, one at a time, along with the lemon zest and vanilla. Beat for 5 minutes until light and fluffy. Cover and refrigerate for 1 hour. Brush each of 2 sheets of fillo thoroughly with melted butter, stack them, and cut into 4 or 5 strips. Place 1 to 1½ tablespoons of the cheese mixture at end of one of the fillo strips. Fold up in the shape of a triangle and continue with the remainder of the cheese mixture and the fillo sheets. Arrange on a greased cookie sheet 1 inch apart, brush the tops with butter, sprinkle with a little water, and bake for 25 to 30 minutes, or until golden brown. Remove from the oven and cool. Dust the top with the confectioners' sugar and cinnamon.

♦ *Yields 2 to 2½ dozen*

Sweet Easter Bread

Tsoureki

Tsoureki is the traditional Greek Sweet Easter bread. The bread is braided, decorated with red eggs, and sprinkled with almond slivers or sesame seeds.

2 cups warm milk

2 level tablespoons brewer's yeast
   or 2 envelopes dry yeast

6 to 7 cups all-purpose flour

2 tablespoons sugar

1¼ cups (2½ sticks) unsalted
   butter, melted

4 large eggs, beaten

1½ cups sugar

2 tablespoons grated lemon zest

2 teaspoons ground mastic or
   2 teaspoons vanilla

4 to 5 dyed red eggs for
   decoration (optional)

2 egg yolks

2 tablespoons milk

½ cup almond slivers or ¼ cup
   sesame seeds, for garnish

In a large bowl, stir the yeast in the milk to dissolve. Stir in 1½ cups flour and 2 tablespoons sugar to make a thick batter. Place the bowl in a warm place and cover with a towel to activate the yeast; let rise for about 1 hour or less. Put about 5 cups of flour in a large bowl; make a well in the middle of the flour and add the melted butter, beaten eggs, 1½ cups of sugar, lemon zest, and mastic or vanilla. Add the yeast mixture, stirring with a wooden spoon, until dough begins to form. Slowly adding more flour if necessary, knead the dough for 10 minutes, or until it is soft and silky. Place in a large greased bowl, cover with a towel, and let rise until the dough doubles in size; this should take about 2 hours. Preheat the oven to 350 degrees. Knead the dough again for 5 minutes and with a sharp knife cut the dough into 6 balls. Roll each into a long strip 10 to 12 inches long.

Lay 3 strips side by side and press one end together. Braid the strips and press them together at the bottom. Make 2 loaves or form the bread into rings. If you choose to decorate with dyed red eggs, press them into the dough. Place on a buttered baking sheet, cover, and let rise until loaves or rings double in size. (It should take about 2 to 2½ hours for dough to double.) In a small bowl, stir the egg yolks and milk. When the bread has risen, brush with egg yolk mixture, then sprinkle with almonds or sesame seeds and bake for 45 to 50 minutes, or until golden brown. Remove from the oven and cool on wire racks.

◆ *Yields 2 loaves*

Note: Mastic can be found in any Greek market.

Traditional Lucky New Year's Sweet Bread

VASSILOPITA

This sweet bread is a tradition in all Greek homes. A coin is put into the dough before baking, and whoever gets the piece with the coin is the lucky one for the New Year. The name, Vassilopita, comes from Saint Vasilius, who symbolizes New Year's.

2 cups plus 2 tablespoons milk

2 level tablespoons brewer's yeast
    or 2 envelopes dry yeast

6 to 7 cups all-purpose flour

1 cup (2 sticks) unsalted butter,
    melted

1½ cups sugar

4 large eggs, beaten

1 tablespoon lemon zest

1 tablespoon orange zest

Juice of 1 orange

2 teaspoons vanilla

1 coin wrapped with aluminum
    foil, to insert before baking

Butter, for greasing the pan

1 egg yolk

2 tablespoons milk

½ cup blanched, skinned, and
    sliced almonds, for topping

Warm 2 cups of milk. Into a large bowl, add the warm milk and yeast and stir to dissolve. Add 1½ cups flour and mix to make a thick batter. Place the bowl in a warm place, cover with a towel, and let the dough rise for about 2 hours. Put about 5 cups of flour in a large bowl make a well in the middle of the flour and add the melted butter, sugar, 4 beaten eggs, lemon zest, orange zest, orange juice, and vanilla. Add the yeast mixture and stir with a wooden spoon until dough begins to form. Slowly adding more flour if necessary, knead the dough for 10 minutes, or until it is soft and silky. Place the dough into a large greased bowl, cover with a towel, and let the dough rise and double in size. (This will take about 2 hours.) Knead the dough again and insert the foil-wrapped coin in it. Butter a 12 × 2-inch round pan. Place the dough in the pan, making sure that it does not fill the pan more than halfway, so the dough will have room to rise. Cover the pan and put it in a warm place until the dough doubles in size, 1½ to 2 hours. Preheat the oven to 350 degrees. Mix the egg yolk with 2 table-spoons of milk, brush on the top of the sweet bread, and sprinkle with almond slices. Bake for 50 minutes, or until golden brown. Remove from the oven and cool on wire rack. You're going to love this sweet bread as much as I do.

♦ *Serves 10 to 12*

INDEX

Greek words are in *italics*.

aginares. See artichokes
almonds
    Orange Cake, 270
    Revani Cake with Yogurt,
      271–72
    Secret Kiss Kourambiethes
      Cookies, 273–74
    Sweet Easter Bread,
      280–81
    Traditional Lucky New
      Year's Sweet Bread,
      282–83
Amalia's Beef Stew, 36
anthotiro cheese, 76
appetizers, 3–4. *See also* dips
    Appetizer Meatballs, 5
    Baked Meat Triangles, 7
    Chicken-Stuffed Grape
      Leaves, 110
    Feta Cheese Triangles, 10
    Garlic Feta Cheese Spread,
      11

Georgia's Garlic Chicken
    Wings, 113
Georgia's Shrimp with
    Feta in Fillo, 26
Georgia's Special Spinach
    Triangles, 12
Grilled Marinated
    Haloumi Cheese, 16
Grilled Octopus, 15
Grilled Saganaki Cheese
    Wrapped in Grape
    Leaves, 13
Marinated Octopus, 18
Marinated Olives, 19
Meze Fried Cheese, 20
Meze Fried Squid, 21
Mussels with Wine, 22
Mykonos Seafood
    Triangles, 23
Olive and Cheese Platter,
    24
Potatoes with Garlic

Sauce, 25
Shrimp with Garlic, 27
Shrimp with Ouzo, 198
Stuffed Grape Leaves with
    Egg Lemon Sauce,
    167–68
Toasted Bread Riganato
    with Tomatoes and
    Feta, 28
Yiayia's Garlic Sauce, 29
arni. See lamb
Aromatic Braised Roast Beef,
    129
Aromatic Grilled Chicken
    with Wine, 104
Aromatic Lamb Kabobs,
    130
Aromatic Lamb with
    Tomato Sauce and
    Pasta, 131
Aromatic Lentil Soup, 37
Aromatic Marinade, 67

artichokes (*aginares*)
Artichoke Feta Cheese
Tart, 237–38
Chickpea Salad, 57
Daisy's Chicken Calzone,
225
Grecian Beef Soup with
Vegetables, 44
Lemon Fava Beans with
Artichokes, 88
Pasta Topped with
Artichokes and Feta, 210
Pizza with Artichokes and
Feta, 229
Pizza with Olives and
Artichokes, 232
Potato and Artichoke
Salad, 58

Baked Fish Spetsiota, 180
Baked Fish Steaks with
Potatoes and Onions,
181
Baked Fish with Peppers and
Feta Cheese, 182–83
Baked Lamb with Potatoes,
132
Baked Lima Butter Beans, 81
Baked Meat Triangles, 7
Baked Potatoes with Onions,
82
beans (*fasolia*)
Baked Lima Butter Beans,
81
Bean Salad, 54
Bean Soup with Leeks,
38
Green Beans with
Zucchini, 87

Lemon Fava Beans with
Artichokes, 88
Lemon White Bean Soup,
46
String Beans with
Potatoes, 94
Béchamel sauce, 209
beef
Amalia's Beef Stew, 36
Appetizer Meatballs, 5
Appetizer Spiced Feta, 6
Aromatic Braised Roast
Beef, 129
Baked Meat Triangles, 7
Calzone Stuffed with
Meat, 222–23
Grecian Beef Soup with
Vegetables, 44
Greek Lasagna, 138–39
Hamburgers Pane, 144
Hamburgers Stuffed with
Feta Cheese, 145
Lasagna Pastitsio with
Fillo Dough, 204–5
Meatballs with Tomato
Sauce, 152–53
Meat Loaf Roll Stuffed
with Eggs, 155
Meat Loaf with Feta
Cheese, 154
Meat Pie with Pine Nuts,
246–47
Moussaka, 156–57
Pizza with Meatballs,
230–31
Spaghetti with Meat
Sauce, 213
Stuffed Cabbage with Egg
Lemon Sauce, 166

Stuffed Cannelloni with
Meat, 215
Stuffed Grape Leaves with
Egg Lemon Sauce,
167–68
Stuffed Romaine Lettuce
with Egg and Lemon
Sauce, 171–72
Stuffed Turkey with
Chestnuts, 123–24
Beet Salad, 55
Black-Eyed Bean Soup, 39
Boiled Cauliflower Salad, 56
brandy, 217
breads
Sweet Easter Bread,
280–81
Traditional Lucky New
Year's Sweet Bread,
282–83
Butter Cookies with
Hazelnuts, 256

cabbage (*laxanopita*)
buying and storage tip, 31
Cabbage Sausage Fillo
Rolls, 239–40
Spiced Pork with Cabbage
in Tomato Sauce, 164
Stuffed Cabbage with Egg
Lemon Sauce, 166
Vegetarian Stuffed
Cabbage with Egg and
Lemon Sauce, 96–97
cakes
Orange Cake, 270
Revani Cake with Yogurt,
271–72
syrup topping tips, 236

calzones (*skaltsounia*)
Calzone Stuffed with
Meat, 222–23
Calzone with Spinach and
Feta Filling, 224
Daisy's Chicken Calzone,
225
cannelloni beans
Bean Salad, 54
Bean Soup with Leeks, 38
Lemon White Bean Soup,
46
casseroles. *See also* lasagna
Chicken Casserole with
Egg Noodles, 105
Delicious Moussaka with
Chicken, 111–12
Moussaka, 156–57
cauliflower (*kounoupithi*)
Boiled Cauliflower Salad,
56
buying and storage tip,
31
Cauliflower Stew with
Onions, 83
caviar (*tarama*)
Greek Caviar Dip, 14
cheese. *See also* feta cheese;
kaseri cheese; kefalotyri
cheese
Cheese Pie, 241
Grilled Marinated
Haloumi Cheese, 16
Peter's Greek-Style Pizza,
227–28
types of, 75–76
chestnuts (*kastana*)
Stuffed Turkey with
Chestnuts, 123–24

chicken (*kota*)
Aromatic Grilled Chicken
with Wine, 104
Chicken Casserole with
Egg Noodles, 105
Chicken Croquettes, 106
Chicken Rice Fillo Rolls,
242–43
Chicken Soup in Egg
Lemon Sauce, 40
Chicken Stew with
Peppers, 107
Chicken Stew with
Potatoes, 108
Chicken Stew with Rice,
109
Chicken-Stuffed Grape
Leaves, 110
Chicken Tomato Soup
with Fides, 41
Daisy's Chicken Calzone,
225
Delicious Moussaka with
Chicken, 111–12
Georgia's Chicken Broth,
43
Georgia's Garlic Chicken
Wings, 113
Grecian Chicken Kabobs
with Vegetables, 114–15
Grilled Chicken Beefteki,
116
Lasagna with Chicken
and Béchamel Sauce,
206–7
Lemon Chicken Noodle
Soup, 45
Lemon Chicken with Pota-
toes, 117

Olympia Egg and Lemon
Chicken Soup, 47
Oven-Fried Chicken
Breasts, 118–19
Potato and Chicken Salad,
59
preparation tip, 32
Roasted Chicken with
Potatoes and Onions,
120
Spaghetti with Ground
Chicken Sauce, 212
Stuffed Chicken with
Mushrooms and Rice,
121–22
Village Chicken Pie,
253–54
chickpeas (*revithia*)
Chickpea Salad, 57
Delicious Chickpea Soup,
42
chocolate
Georgia's Chocolate
Cream Cheese Cake,
262–63
Secret Kiss
Kourambiethes
Cookies, 273–74
Classic Lamb Rolls with
Fillo Dough, 244–45
cookies
Butter Cookies with
Hazelnuts, 256
Cookie Twists, 257
Secret Kiss Kourambiethes
Cookies, 273–74
Stuffed Melomakarona
Honey-Dunked Cookies,
277–78

Copenhagen Walnut and
Fillo Dough Pastry,
258–59
Corfu Spicy Veal Stew with
Pasta, 133
crabmeat
Mykonos Seafood Trian-
gles, 23
cream cheese
Georgia's Cheesecake
Baklava, 260–61
Georgia's Chocolate
Cream Cheese Cake,
262–63
Sweet Cream Cheese Fillo
Triangles, 279
cucumbers
Cucumber Yogurt Dip, 8
Tomato and Cucumber
Salad, 61

Daisy's Chicken Calzone, 225
Delicious Chickpea Soup, 42
Delicious Moussaka with
Chicken, 111–12
Delicious Pork Kabobs, 134
Delicious Pork with Leeks,
135
desserts. *See also* cakes;
cookies
Copenhagen Walnut and
Fillo Dough Pastry,
258–59
Georgia's Cheesecake
Baklava, 260–61
Georgia's Chocolate Cream
Cheese Cake, 262–63
Georgia's Famous Baklava
with Olive Oil, 264–65

Honey Fritters, 266–67
Semolina Pudding with
Raisins and Pine Nuts,
275–76
Sweet Cream Cheese Fillo
Triangles, 279
dips
Cucumber Yogurt Dip, 8
Eggplant Dip with
Yogurt, 9
Greek Caviar Dip, 14
Kalamata Olive Dip, 17
dolmathakia. See grape leaves
dressings
Oil, Lemon, and Garlic
Dressing, 70
A Touch of Georgia's
Dressing, 66
dyed eggs for Easter, 125

eggplants (*melizanes*)
Delicious Moussaka with
Chicken, 111–12
Eggplant Dip with
Yogurt, 9
Eggplant Ragout, 84
Fried Eggplant with
Tomato Sauce, 85–86
Moussaka, 156–57
eggs
Chicken Soup in Egg
Lemon Sauce, 40
dyed eggs for Easter, 125
Egg and lemon sauce, 97
Egg lemon sauce, 40,
149–50, 167–68, 171–72
Lamb with Spinach and
Egg Lemon Sauce,
149–50

Meat Loaf Roll Stuffed
with Eggs, 155
Olympia Egg and Lemon
Chicken Soup, 47
Stuffed Cabbage with Egg
Lemon Sauce, 166
Stuffed Grape Leaves with
Egg Lemon Sauce,
167–68
Stuffed Romaine Lettuce
with Egg and Lemon
Sauce, 171–72
Vegetarian Stuffed
Cabbage with Egg and
Lemon Sauce, 96–97
elitses. See olives

fasolia. See beans
fava beans
Lemon Fava Beans with
Artichokes, 88
fennel
Spinach and Feta Cheese
Tarts, 248
Spinach Pie, 249–50
feta cheese, 75
Appetizer Spiced Feta, 6
Artichoke Feta Cheese
Tart, 237–38
Baked Fish with Peppers
and Feta Cheese,
182–83
Calzone with Spinach and
Feta Filling, 224
Cheese Pie, 241
Chicken Rice Fillo Rolls,
242–43
Daisy's Chicken Calzone,
225

Feta Cheese Triangles, 10
Garlic Feta Cheese
    Spread, 11
Georgia's Shrimp with
    Feta in Fillo, 26
Georgia's Special Spinach
    Triangles, 12
Grecian Chicken Kabobs
    with Vegetables,
    114–15
Grilled Lamb Chops
    Stuffed with Feta
    Cheese, 140–41
Hamburgers Stuffed with
    Feta Cheese, 145
Lasagna with Leeks and
    Béchamel Sauce, 208–9
Meat Loaf with Feta
    Cheese, 154
Mykonos Seafood
    Triangles, 23
Pasta Topped with
    Artichokes and Feta, 210
Pizza with Artichokes and
    Feta, 229
Pizza with Spinach and
    Feta, 233
Shrimp Saganaki with
    Feta Cheese, 197
Spinach and Feta Cheese
    Tarts, 248
Spinach Pie, 249–50
Tart with Shrimp and
    Feta Cheese, 251–52
Toasted Bread Riganato
    with Tomatoes and
    Feta, 28
Village Chicken Pie,
    253–54

fillo dishes, savory
    Baked Meat Triangles, 7
    Cabbage Sausage Fillo
        Rolls, 239–40
    Cheese Pie, 241
    Chicken Rice Fillo Rolls,
        242–43
    Classic Lamb Rolls with
        Fillo Dough, 244–45
    Feta Cheese Triangles, 10
    Georgia's Shrimp with
        Feta in Fillo, 26
    Georgia's Special Spinach
        Triangles, 12
    Lasagna Pastitsio with
        Fillo Dough, 204–5
    Meat Pie with Pine Nuts,
        246–47
    Mykonos Seafood Trian-
        gles, 23
    Spinach Pie, 249–50
    Village Chicken Pie,
        253–54
fillo dishes, sweet
    Copenhagen Walnut and
        Fillo Dough Pastry,
        258–59
    Georgia's Cheesecake
        Baklava, 260–61
    Georgia's Famous Baklava
        with Olive Oil, 264–65
    Kataifi Shredded Fillo
        Pastry with Walnuts
        and Pistachio Nuts,
        268–69
    Sweet Cream Cheese Fillo
        Triangles, 279
fillo dough directions and
    tips, 201–2

fish (*psari*)
    Baked Fish Spetsiota, 180
    Baked Fish Steaks with
        Potatoes and Onions,
        181
    Baked Fish with Peppers
        and Feta Cheese, 182–83
    Fried Fish, 184
    Fried Salted Cod, 185
    Georgia's Stuffed
        Haddock, 186
    Grilled Salmon, 187
    Grilled Sardines with
        Garlic and Lemon
        Sauce, 188
    Grilled Sardines with
        Grape Leaves, 189
    Grilled Seafood Kabobs,
        190–91
    Grilled Swordfish Kabobs
        with Bay Leaves, 192
    Lemon Fried Red Mullet,
        193
    Marinated Baked
        Mackerel, 195
Fried Eggplant with Tomato
    Sauce, 85–86
Fried Fish, 184
Fried Salted Cod, 185

galopoula. *See* turkey
garides. *See* shrimp
Garlic and Basil Pizza, 226
Garlic Feta Cheese Spread, 11
Georgia's Cheesecake
    Baklava, 260–61
Georgia's Chicken Broth, 43
Georgia's Chocolate Cream
    Cheese Cake, 262–63

Georgia's Famous Baklava with Olive Oil, 264–65
Georgia's Garlic Chicken Wings, 113
Georgia's Roasted Leg of Lamb, 136–37
Georgia's Shrimp with Feta in Fillo, 26
Georgia's Special Spinach Triangles, 12
Georgia's Stuffed Haddock, 186
Georgia-Style Béchamel Sauce, 68
grape leaves
    Chicken-Stuffed Grape Leaves, 110
    Grilled Sardines with Grape Leaves, 189
    Stuffed Grape Leaves with Egg Lemon Sauce, 167–68
    Vegetarian Stuffed Grape Leaves with Rice, 98
Grecian Beef Soup with Vegetables, 44
Grecian Chicken Kabobs with Vegetables, 114–15
Greek Caviar Dip, 14
Greek ingredients
    brandy, 217
    cheese types, 75–76
    herbs and spices, 49–52
    mastiha, 218
    olive types, 63–64
    ouzo, 217
    wine, 218–19
Greek Lasagna, 138–39

Green Beans with Zucchini, 87
Grilled Chicken Beefteki, 116
Grilled Lamb Chops Stuffed with Feta Cheese, 140–41
Grilled Lamb Chops with mint Marinade, 142
Grilled Marinated Haloumi Cheese, 16
Grilled Octopus, 15
Grilled or Broiled Pork Chops, 143
Grilled Saganaki Cheese Wrapped in Grape Leaves, 13
Grilled Salmon, 187
Grilled Sardines with Garlic and Lemon Sauce, 188
Grilled Sardines with Grape Leaves, 189
Grilled Seafood Kabobs, 190–91
Grilled Swordfish Kabobs with Bay Leaves, 192
Gruyère cheese, 76

haloumi cheese, 76
    Grilled Marinated Haloumi Cheese, 16
ham
    Georgia's Shrimp with Feta in Fillo, 26
    Stuffed Leg of Lamb with Ham and Cheese, 169–70
Hamburgers Pane, 144
Hamburgers Stuffed with Feta Cheese, 145

hazelnuts
    Butter Cookies with Hazelnuts, 256
herbs and spices, 49–52
Honey Fritters, 266–67

kalamari. See squid
Kalamata Olive Dip, 17
kaseri cheese, 76
    Calzone Stuffed with Meat, 222–23
    Garlic and Basil Pizza, 226
    Peter's Greek-Style Pizza, 227–28
    Pizza with Meatballs, 230–31
    Pizza with Olives and Artichokes, 232
    Shrimp Pizza, 234
kastana. See chestnuts
Kataifi Shredded Fillo Pastry with Walnuts and Pistachio Nuts, 268–69
kefalograviera cheese, 76
kefalotyri cheese, 75
    Calzone with Spinach and Feta Filling, 224
    Cheese Pie, 241
    Classic Lamb Rolls with Fillo Dough, 244–45
    Delicious Moussaka with Chicken, 111–12
    Fried Eggplant with Tomato Sauce, 85–86
    Greek Lasagna, 138–39
    Grilled Saganaki Cheese Wrapped in Grape Leaves, 13

Lasagna Pastitsio with
Fillo Dough, 204–5
Lasagna with Chicken and
Béchamel Sauce, 206–7
Lasagna with Leeks and
Béchamel Sauce, 208–9
Meze Fried Cheese, 20
Olive and Cheese Platter,
24
Stuffed Cannelloni with
Meat, 215
Stuffed Leg of Lamb with
Ham and Cheese,
169–70
kolokithakia. See zucchini
kota. See chicken
kounoupithi. See cauliflower
ktapodi. See octopus

lamb (*arni*)
Aromatic Lamb Kabobs,
130
Aromatic Lamb with
Tomato Sauce and
Pasta, 131
Baked Lamb with
Potatoes, 132
Classic Lamb Rolls with
Fillo Dough, 244–45
Georgia's Roasted Leg of
Lamb, 136–37
Grilled Lamb Chops
Stuffed with Feta
Cheese, 140–41
Grilled Lamb Chops with
Mint Marinade, 142
Lamb Chops Pane, 146–47
Lamb Ragout with Pota-
toes, 148

Lamb with Spinach and
Egg Lemon Sauce,
149–50
Oven-Baked Lamb with
Zucchini, 158
Roasted Rack of Lamb
with Lemon, 162
Stove-Top Roasted Lamb
with Lemon, 165
Stuffed Leg of Lamb with
Ham and Cheese,
169–70
lasagna (*pastitsio*)
Greek Lasagna, 138–39
Lasagna Pastitsio with
Fillo Dough, 204–5
Lasagna with Chicken
and Béchamel Sauce,
206–7
Lasagna with Leeks and
Béchamel Sauce, 208–9
laxanopita. See cabbage
leeks (*prasa*)
Bean Soup with Leeks, 38
Black-Eyed Bean Soup, 39
Delicious Pork with Leeks,
135
Lasagna with Leeks and
Béchamel Sauce, 208–9
lemons
Chicken Soup in Egg
Lemon Sauce, 40
Egg and lemon sauce, 97
Egg lemon sauce, 40,
149–50, 167–68, 171–72
Garlic lemon sauce, 188
Grilled Sardines with
Garlic and Lemon
Sauce, 188

Lamb with Spinach and
Egg Lemon Sauce,
149–50
Lemon Chicken Noodle
Soup, 45
Lemon Chicken with Pota-
toes, 117
Lemon Fava Beans with
Artichokes, 88
Lemon Fried Red Mullet,
193
Lemon Garlic Roasted
Pork Loin, 151
Lemon Grilled Lobster
Tails, 194
Lemon marinade, 160
Lemon Roast Potatoes,
89
Lemon White Bean Soup,
46
Olympia Egg and Lemon
Chicken Soup, 47
Rice with Spinach and
Lemon, 93
Roasted Rack of Lamb
with Lemon, 162
Stove-Top Roasted Lamb
with Lemon, 165
Stuffed Cabbage with Egg
Lemon Sauce, 166
Stuffed Grape Leaves with
Egg Lemon Sauce,
167–68
Stuffed Romaine Lettuce
with Egg and Lemon
Sauce, 171–72
Vegetarian Stuffed
Cabbage with Egg and
Lemon Sauce, 96–97

lentils
  Aromatic Lentil Soup, 37
lima beans. *See* beans
lobster
  Lemon Grilled Lobster
    Tails, 194
loukaniko. See sausage

Margarita's Tomato Sauce,
    69
marinades (*marinara*)
  Aromatic Marinade, 67
  for chicken, 104, 114, 118,
    120
  for fish and seafood, 190,
    192
  for lamb, 130, 136,
    140–41, 146, 169–70
  Lemon marinade, 160
  Ouzo Marinade for Grilled
    Steaks, 71
  for pork, 134, 143
  Rosemary Marinade, 72
  for shrimp, 196
  Wine Marinade for Beef or
    Lamb Kabobs, 73
Marinated Baked Mackerel,
    195
Marinated Octopus, 18
Marinated Olives, 19
marouli. See romaine lettuce
mastiha, 218
Meatballs with Tomato
    Sauce, 152–53
Meatless Stuffed Peppers and
    Tomatoes with Rice,
    90–91
Meat Loaf Roll Stuffed with
    Eggs, 155

Meat Loaf with Feta Cheese,
    154
Meat Pie with Pine Nuts,
    246–47
melizanes. See eggplant
meze. See appetizers
Meze Fried Cheese, 20
Meze Fried Squid, 21
mizithra cheese, 76
Moussaka, 156–57
mushrooms
  Calzone Stuffed with
    Meat, 222–23
  Spaghetti with Meat
    Sauce, 213
  Stuffed Chicken with
    Mushrooms and Rice,
    121–22
  Tart with Shrimp and
    Feta Cheese, 251–52
  Village Chicken Pie,
    253–54
Mussels with Wine, 22
Mykonos Grilled Shrimp
    Souvlaki, 196
Mykonos Seafood Triangles,
    23
My Mother's Village-Style
    Veal Soup, 48

octopus (*ktapodi*)
  Grilled Octopus, 15
  Marinated Octopus, 18
Oil, Lemon, and Garlic
    Dressing, 70
olive oil, 32, 100–102
olives (*elitses*)
  Daisy's Chicken Calzone,
    225

Kalamata Olive Dip, 17
Marinated Olives, 19
Olive and Cheese Platter,
    24
Pasta Topped with
    Artichokes and Feta, 210
Pizza with Olives and
    Artichokes, 232
  types of, 63–64
Olympia Egg and Lemon
    Chicken Soup, 47
Olympic Games, 175–77
onions
  Amalia's Beef Stew, 36
  Baked Fish Steaks with
    Potatoes and Onions,
    181
  Baked Potatoes with
    Onions, 82
  Cauliflower Stew with
    Onions, 83
  Delicious Pork Kabobs,
    134
  Grilled Seafood Kabobs,
    190–91
  Roasted Chicken with
    Potatoes and Onions,
    120
  Sausage with Peppers and
    Onions, 163
Orange Cake, 270
ouzo, 217
  Butter Cookies with
    Hazelnuts, 256
  Ouzo Marinade for Grilled
    Steaks, 71
  Shrimp with Ouzo, 198
Oven-Baked Lamb with
    Zucchini, 158

Oven-Fried Chicken Breasts, 118–19

pasta
Aromatic Lamb with Tomato Sauce and Pasta, 131
Chicken Casserole with Egg Noodles, 105
Corfu Spicy Veal Stew with Pasta, 133
Greek Lasagna, 138–39
Lasagna Pastitsio with Fillo Dough, 204–5
Lasagna with Chicken and Béchamel Sauce, 206–7
Lasagna with Leeks and Béchamel Sauce, 208–9
Pasta Topped with Artichokes and Feta, 210
Spaghetti with Ground Chicken Sauce, 212
Spaghetti with Meat Sauce, 213
Spaghetti with Tomato Sauce, 214
Stuffed Cannelloni with Meat, 215
pastitsio. See lasagna
Pastry crust, 251–52
pastry tips, 236
patates. See potatoes
peppers (*pipergies*)
Baked Fish with Peppers and Feta Cheese, 182–83
buying and storage tip, 33
Chicken Stew with Peppers, 107

Delicious Pork Kabobs, 134
Garlic Feta Cheese Spread, 11
Grecian Chicken Kabobs with Vegetables, 114–15
Grilled Seafood Kabobs, 190–91
Meatless Stuffed Peppers and Tomatoes with Rice, 90–91
Sausage with Peppers and Onions, 163
Peter's Greek-Style Pizza, 227–28
pies and tarts
Artichoke Feta Cheese Tart, 237–38
Cheese Pie, 241
Meat Pie with Pine Nuts, 246–47
Pastry crust, 251–52
pastry tips, 236
Spinach and Feta Cheese Tarts, 248
Spinach Pie, 249–50
Tart with Shrimp and Feta Cheese, 251–52
pine nuts
Semolina Pudding with Raisins and Pine Nuts, 275–76
Stuffed Chicken with Mushrooms and Rice, 121–22
Stuffed Turkey with Chestnuts, 123–24
Vegetarian Stuffed

Cabbage with Egg and Lemon Sauce, 96–97
Vegetarian Stuffed Grape Leaves with Rice, 98
pipergies. See peppers
pistachio nuts
Kataifi Shredded Fillo Pastry with Walnuts and Pistachio Nuts, 268–69
pizza
Garlic and Basil Pizza, 226
Peter's Greek-Style Pizza, 227–28
Pizza Dough, 223
Pizza with Artichokes and Feta, 229
Pizza with Meatballs, 230–31
Pizza with Olives and Artichokes, 232
Pizza with Spinach and Feta, 233
Shrimp Pizza, 234
pork (*xirino*)
Delicious Pork Kabobs, 134
Delicious Pork with Leeks, 135
Grilled or Broiled Pork Chops, 143
Lemon Garlic Roasted Pork Loin, 151
Meatballs with Tomato Sauce, 152–53
Meat Loaf with Feta Cheese, 154
Pork Fricassee, 159
Roasted Pork with Potatoes, 160–61

pork (*xirino*) (*continued*)
  Spiced Pork with Cabbage
    in Tomato Sauce, 164
potatoes (*patates*)
  Baked Fish Steaks with
    Potatoes and Onions,
    181
  Baked Lamb with
    Potatoes, 132
  Baked Potatoes with
    Onions, 82
  buying and storage tip, 33
  Chicken Stew with
    Potatoes, 108
  Grecian Beef Soup with
    Vegetables, 44
  Greek Caviar Dip, 14
  Lamb Ragout with Pota-
    toes, 148
  Lemon Chicken with Pota-
    toes, 117
  Lemon Roast Potatoes, 89
  Meatless Stuffed Peppers
    and Tomatoes with
    Rice, 90–91
  My Mother's Village-Style
    Veal Soup, 48
  Potato and Artichoke
    Salad, 58
  Potato and Chicken Salad,
    59
  Potatoes with Garlic
    Sauce, 25
  Potatoes Yiahni, 92
  Roasted Chicken with
    Potatoes and Onions,
    120
  Roasted Pork with
    Potatoes, 160–61

String Beans with
  Potatoes, 94
Village Chicken Pie,
  253–54
prasa. See leeks
psari. See fish

raisins
  Semolina Pudding with
    Raisins and Pine Nuts,
    275–76
  Revani Cake with Yogurt,
    271–72
revithia. See chickpeas
rice (*rizi*)
  Chicken Rice Fillo Rolls,
    242–43
  Chicken Soup in Egg
    Lemon Sauce, 40
  Chicken Stew with Rice,
    109
  Chicken-Stuffed Grape
    Leaves, 110
  Grecian Chicken Kabobs
    with Vegetables,
    114–15
  Meatless Stuffed Peppers
    and Tomatoes with
    Rice, 90–91
  Rice Pilaf with Vegetables,
    211
  Rice with Spinach and
    Lemon, 93
  Stuffed Cabbage with
    Egg Lemon Sauce,
    166
  Stuffed Chicken with
    Mushrooms and Rice,
    121–22

Stuffed Grape Leaves with
  Egg Lemon Sauce,
  167–68
Stuffed Romaine Lettuce
  with Egg and Lemon
  Sauce, 171–72
Stuffed Squid with Rice,
  199–200
Stuffed Turkey with
  Chestnuts, 123–24
Stuffed Zucchini with
  Rice, 95
Tomato Rice Pilaf, 216
Veal Stew with Rice Pilaf,
  173
Vegetarian Stuffed
  Cabbage with Egg and
  Lemon Sauce, 96–97
Vegetarian Stuffed Grape
  Leaves with Rice, 98
Roasted Chicken with Pota-
  toes and Onions, 120
Roasted Pork with Potatoes,
  160–61
Roasted Rack of Lamb with
  Lemon, 162
romaine lettuce (*marouli*)
  buying and storage tip, 32
  Pork Fricassee, 159
  Romaine Lettuce Salad, 60
  Stuffed Romaine Lettuce
    with Egg and Lemon
    Sauce, 171–72
Rosemary Marinade, 72

salad dressings. *See* dressings
salads (*salata*)
  Bean Salad, 54
  Beet Salad, 55

Boiled Cauliflower Salad, 56
Chickpea Salad, 57
Potato and Artichoke Salad, 58
Potato and Chicken Salad, 59
Romaine Lettuce Salad, 60
Tomato and Cucumber Salad, 61
Zucchini Salad, 62
sardines. *See* fish
sauces (*saltsa*)
Béchamel sauce, 209
Egg and lemon sauce, 97
Egg lemon sauce, 40, 149–50, 167–68, 171–72
Garlic lemon sauce, 188
Georgia-Style Béchamel Sauce, 68
Margarita's Tomato Sauce, 69
Tomato Sauce, 152–53, 227, 230, 234
Yiayia's Garlic Sauce, 29
sausage (*loukaniko*)
Cabbage Sausage Fillo Rolls, 239–40
Sausage with Peppers and Onions, 163
scallops
Grilled Seafood Kabobs, 190–91
Secret Kiss Kourambiethes Cookies, 273–74
Semolina Pudding with Raisins and Pine Nuts, 275–76
shrimp (*garides*)

Georgia's Shrimp with Feta in Fillo, 26
Grilled Seafood Kabobs, 190–91
Mykonos Grilled Shrimp Souvlaki, 196
Mykonos Seafood Triangles, 23
Shrimp Pizza, 234
Shrimp Saganaki with Feta Cheese, 197
Shrimp with Garlic, 27
Shrimp with Ouzo, 198
Tart with Shrimp and Feta Cheese, 251–52
skaltsounia. See calzones
soups (*soupa*), 33. *See also* stews
Aromatic Lentil Soup, 37
Bean Soup with Leeks, 38
Black-Eyed Bean Soup, 39
Chicken Soup in Egg Lemon Sauce, 40
Chicken Tomato Soup with Fides, 41
Delicious Chickpea Soup, 42
Georgia's Chicken Broth, 43
Grecian Beef Soup with Vegetables, 44
Lemon Chicken Noodle Soup, 45
Lemon White Bean Soup, 46
My Mother's Village-Style Veal Soup, 48
Olympia Egg and Lemon Chicken Soup, 47

Spaghetti with Ground Chicken Sauce, 212
Spaghetti with Meat Sauce, 213
Spaghetti with Tomato Sauce, 214
spanaki. See spinach
Spiced Pork with Cabbage in Tomato Sauce, 164
spinach (*spanaki*)
buying and storage tip, 33
Calzone with Spinach and Feta Filling, 224
Georgia's Special Spinach Triangles, 12
Lamb with Spinach and Egg Lemon Sauce, 149–50
Pizza with Spinach and Feta, 233
Rice with Spinach and Lemon, 93
Spinach and Feta Cheese Tarts, 248
Spinach Pie, 249–50
squid (*kalamari*)
Meze Fried Squid, 21
Stuffed Squid with Rice, 199–200
stews. *See also* soups
Amalia's Beef Stew, 36
Chicken Stew with Peppers, 107
Chicken Stew with Potatoes, 108
Chicken Stew with Rice, 109
Corfu Spicy Veal Stew with Pasta, 133

stews (*continued*)

    Veal Stew with Rice Pilaf, 173

Stove-Top Roasted Lamb with Lemon, 165

String Beans with Potatoes, 94

Stuffed Cabbage with Egg Lemon Sauce, 166

Stuffed Cannelloni with Meat, 215

Stuffed Chicken with Mushrooms and Rice, 121–22

Stuffed Grape Leaves with Egg Lemon Sauce, 167–68

Stuffed Leg of Lamb with Ham and Cheese, 169–70

Stuffed Melomakarona Honey-Dunked Cookies, 277–78

Stuffed Romaine Lettuce with Egg and Lemon Sauce, 171–72

Stuffed Squid with Rice, 199–200

Stuffed Turkey with Chestnuts, 123–24

Stuffed Zucchini with Rice, 95

Sweet Cream Cheese Fillo Triangles, 279

Sweet Easter Bread, 280–81

swordfish. *See* fish

Syrup, 259, 261, 265, 266, 269, 272, 275, 278

syrup topping tips, 236

tarama. See caviar

tarts. *See* pies and tarts

Tart with Shrimp and Feta Cheese, 251–52

tips, general food, 31–34

Toasted Bread Riganato with Tomatoes and Feta, 28

tomatoes (*tomata*)

    Aromatic Lamb with Tomato Sauce and Pasta, 131

    Baked Lima Butter Beans, 81

    buying and storage tip, 33

    Chicken Tomato Soup with Fides, 41

    Delicious Pork Kabobs, 134

    Fried Eggplant with Tomato Sauce, 85–86

    Grecian Chicken Kabobs with Vegetables, 114–15

    Grilled Seafood Kabobs, 190–91

    Margarita's Tomato Sauce, 69

    Meatballs with Tomato Sauce, 152–53

    Meatless Stuffed Peppers and Tomatoes with Rice, 90–91

    Spaghetti with Tomato Sauce, 214

    Spiced Pork with Cabbage in Tomato Sauce, 164

    Toasted Bread Riganato with Tomatoes and Feta, 28

    Tomato and Cucumber Salad, 61

    Tomato Rice Pilaf, 216

    Tomato Sauce, 152–53, 227, 230, 234

A Touch of Georgia's Dressing, 66

Traditional Lucky New Year's Sweet Bread, 282–83

turkey (*galopoula*)

    Stuffed Turkey with Chestnuts, 123–24

tzatziki. See Cucumber Yogurt Dip

veal

    Corfu Spicy Veal Stew with Pasta, 133

    My Mother's Village-Style Veal Soup, 48

    Veal Stew with Rice Pilaf, 173

vegetables, 80. *See also specific vegetables*

    buying and storage tips, 31–34

    Rice Pilaf with Vegetables, 211

    Vegetarian Stuffed Cabbage with Egg and Lemon Sauce, 96–97

    Vegetarian Stuffed Grape Leaves with Rice, 98

Village Chicken Pie, 253–54

walnuts

    Copenhagen Walnut and Fillo Dough Pastry, 258–59

    Georgia's Cheesecake Baklava, 260–61

Georgia's Famous
Baklava with Olive Oil,
264–65
Kataifi Shredded Fillo
Pastry with Walnuts
and Pistachio Nuts,
268–69
Stuffed Melomakarona
Honey-Dunked Cookies,
277–78
Yiayia's Garlic Sauce, 29
white beans. *See* cannelloni
beans
wine
Amalia's Beef Stew, 36
Aromatic Grilled Chicken
with Wine, 104

Corfu Spicy Veal Stew
with Pasta, 133
Mussels with Wine, 22
types of, 218–19
Wine Marinade for Beef
or Lamb Kabobs, 73

xirino. See pork

Yiayia's Garlic Sauce, 29
yogurt
Cucumber Yogurt Dip,
8
Eggplant Dip with
Yogurt, 9
Revani Cake with Yogurt,
271–72

zucchini (*kolokithakia*)
buying and storage tip,
33
Grecian Chicken Kabobs
with Vegetables,
114–15
Green Beans with
Zucchini, 87
My Mother's Village-
Style Veal Soup,
48
Oven-Baked Lamb with
Zucchini, 158
Stuffed Zucchini with
Rice, 95
Zucchini Ragout, 99
Zucchini Salad, 62